PARENT WIN

*Essential Activities
To Nurture Smarter Kids*

THE FIRST YEAR

Chris Drew, Ph.D.

Werd Factory Books

This non-fiction work is based on research from the fields of early childhood education, early childhood development, literacy studies, cognitive science, and the author's own expertise as a scholar, educator, and parent. Some identities within this work have been anonymized and the creative use of objects, products, etc. do not necessarily indicate an endorsement or safe/intended use of objects. Always be safe and contact your physician about your child's dietary needs and general health and well-being.

Parent Win: Essential Activities to Nurture Smarter Kids, The First Year

ISBN-13: 978-0-9994198-0-9
ISBN-10: 0-9994198-0-3

Library of Congress Control Number: 2017914916

Cover Photography: Serhiy Kobyakov/Shutterstock.com

Werd Factory Books
Silicon Valley, CA, U.S.A.

Contact the Author at:
Chris.Drew.Books@gmail.com

To the awe-inspiring Moms in my life:
Maxine, Bonnie, Kelley, Kassie, and
my wife, Kristin

ACKNOWLEDGMENTS

In many ways, *Parent Win: Essential Activities to Nurture Smarter Kids, The First Year* continues to be a family endeavor. My Mom is the sun to our familial solar system, without whom nothing else exists that is below or before. My sisters, Kelley and Kassie, are two of the most stubbornly determined, intelligent, giving sisters and beautiful moms I have ever seen. Without their direct input and support, this child development guide would not exist.

For nearly a decade, I have been fortunate to work with some of the most highly regarded early childhood education organizations, developmental experts, leading universities, researchers, and scholars in this field. Their early input and contributions have helped infuse rigor to the fun, easy, quirky activities in this program.

Over the years, there have been thousands of families who were part of the Pocket Literacy Coach / Parent University community. Those communities were the digital predecessors to this collection of books. Their intensive responses and inspiring feedback were the fuel to my fire during times when the lights of this project began to dim.

"Chris Drew takes complex, evidence-based research and translates it into simple, do-able activity suggestions that even sleep-deprived parents can do! This is a great source for parents to get easy ideas of how to support healthy infant development."

> ~ Alexis R. Lauricella, Ph.D., Associate Director, Center on Media and Human Development, Northwestern University

"This book brings simplicity, focus, and balance to motherhood. In a society where motherhood can seem like a race or a competition, this book is a reminder of how to live joyfully, simply, balanced and focused on what's important in a precious time of motherhood."

> ~ Kassie Redmond, Middle School Teacher and mother of three, Kansas City, MO

"The whole family wins with *Parent Win*! From enriching my child, to strengthening my relationship with my partner, to committing to my self-care, *Parent Win* has offered deeply meaningful activities that I could incorporate simply and effectively in my daily life."

> ~ Laura P., Mom to Audrey, Los Altos, CA

"In a world with ever-competing priorities, *Parent Win*'s easy, high-impact activities were perfect for us! I feel more bonded to my daughter and more confident as a parent. I am helping her develop every step of the way."

> ~ Kristin B., Mom to Katherine, New York, NY

"I have been following along on the 8 month section since that's Holly's age right now. *LOVE IT!* The concept of a simple activity a day makes it feel so approachable and achievable :) "

> ~ Marlene B., First time Mom to Holly, Walnut Creek, CA

Praise for PARENT WIN: The First Year

"I really enjoyed your book! As a mother, grandmother and a former teacher, the ideas, principles and the simple daily actions discussed in your book really brought into perspective how the simplest of actions can have a monumental effect upon your child! Thanks for pointing this out!"
~ Bonnie W., Grandmother to six and mother of four, Springfield, IL

"*Parent Win* has given me the guidance I need and the confidence to know that I am the best possible parent to my baby girl by giving her all the stimulation, love, and care that I can."
~ Austin W., Mom to Elliot, Burlingame, CA

"In a world where so many parenting books provide theoretical and sometimes overwhelming ideas, thank you for writing a wonderful book with concrete actions that I can take to be a better parent. Every day, I open my book and find something that is achievable, fun for my baby and I, good for our relationship and her development. Thank you!"
~ Jamie K., Mom to Lori, Philadelphia, PA

"First, really cool concept and execution overall! I'm loving the structure, as it is succinct, simple and seemingly manageable to take on from a new mom's perspective."
~ Laura B., Mom to Lilly, San Carlos, CA

"The day we brought *Parent Win* home, my wife and I went through it. We love the format of one activity per day. The format was super-accessible."
~ Frank M., First time Dad to Mateo, San Francisco, CA

"*Parent Win* is a game changer! This spectacular book will help parents develop the confidence and competencies to help their children succeed. A must read for every parent!
~Yolie Flores, MSW, LAUSD Board Member (Ret.)

Chris Drew, Ph.D.

I am grateful to the groups of concerned and educated mothers who have empowered my research for the past several years. In particular, the Mom Group with Laura, Emily, Marlene, Austin, Kristin who have provided invaluable inputs on the manuscript. The influence and importance of the Mom community is truly transformational. And more than their feedback the support and sense of community these friends have provided our family has been nothing short of sanity-saving. If you've ever heard the expression "It takes a village..." and are unsure what it refers to, connect with a moms group in your community and watch the moms and their children flourish.

What was life like before my daughter Madison? Well, as it turns out, I remember it pretty well. All the mountains climbed, cities traveled, beers tasted, workouts completed, free times enjoyed... It is my hope that I can continue to trade those adventures for the life I have now with my two ladies. My baby's hugs, her kisses, her screams, and her fits... I'll take 'em all over any glaciated summit or perfectly crafted brew. She is the one who reminded me of this important work and inspired me to get back to it.

"Baby, looking at you right now there ain't never been no doubt - without you I'd be nothing." I love that country western lyric from Dierks Bentley. It's a poetic way of summing up that which seems to be true for most men, but is especially true in spades when it comes to my marriage: I "married up". One cannot tally the ways in which my life has changed for the better since meeting Kristin. I am better at life than I have ever been or ever could be because of her. And it's not because of some improvement I have made. The single greatest achievement of my life was marrying my wife.

~ Chris Drew, PhD.

PARENT WIN

Essential Activities
To Nurture Smarter Kids

THE FIRST YEAR

INTRODUCTION

As parents, we often feel like there's more we could be doing for our newborns. Compounding this feeling of angst is the reality that we don't always know what the "more" is that we should be doing. The fact that you're curious or concerned is a sure-fire sign that you love and care deeply about your child. And there is nothing in these early months more important than that.

Love is critical. We also want our children to be developing cognitively, physiologically, socially, and emotionally. And as parents we want to know that the actions we are taking towards these ends are impactful. We want to know we're doing the right thing. I started on the journey of writing this book for all these reasons, and more.

The activities in this book are the result of years of researching, testing, and sharing the content in the pages below. Some of the leading early childhood education experts in the world have vetted these activities to be used in some of the premier preschools across the United States. And guess what? There is research that proves the positive impact of doing the activities in this book with your children.

So what do these activities look like? First, we have grouped activities by month. Second, each month has at least one or two themes. For example, one week may focus on bonding with your baby. We know that in the early weeks and months that skin-to-skin contact is an important part of bonding, so the activities focus on things to do that remind and encourage skin-to-skin holding and bonding. Another week may focus on fine motor skills, language skills, listening skills, and so on.

Third, the themes of the activities in each month correspond approximately with the developmental period of your child's life. I say "approximately" because no child develops the same way as the next child. For example, our baby was born a month before her due date. So naturally she had some catching up to do with some things as simple as eating and gaining weight. This, of course, had an impact on how other aspects of her development progressed. Especially early on, we had to constantly remind ourselves not to compare Madison to other babies in our family and circle of friends.

Fourth, many of the activities are designed as much for mom and dad as they are for your little one. I've also written the activities in a way that empowers you to leverage the things in your house, yard, or immediate surrounding. These activities do not require you to go out and buy a new toy or download a new app. So have fun, keep it light, and don't over-complicate things. And don't worry about running out of things to do; there are enough activities to last an entire year!

Chris Drew, Ph.D.

RESEARCH and the PARENT WIN PHILOSOPHY

Parent Win was built on a philosophy that emerged from my research on learning and coaching. That philosophy: *Small acts performed well, repeatedly and over time, is the foundation for excellence* (aka the "small acts" philosophy).

The reasons I focused on early childhood education, which is considered to be the early years of 0-5, are fourfold:

    1. 90% of brain development occurs during the first five years of life
    2. most students who enter kindergarten behind their peers never catch up
    3. the majority of students entering kindergarten are unprepared
    4. parents are a critical part of an untapped portion of education infrastructure

Once I started my dive into research on cognitive development and early childhood education, the *Parent Win* concept became more and more obvious. What wasn't obvious, though, was how to reach 0-5 year olds. For example, most families (over 70% according to available data) do not have access to high quality early childhood care and education opportunities for their 0-5 year olds.

This is just one of the reasons so many (over 50% according to various reports) kindergarteners start school unprepared and behind their peers. This being the case, I determined that activating a part of the education infrastructure that is traditionally disempowered – families – was the richest and most effective opportunity for scaling impact. Caregivers, too, became an important focus. Why? Many people do not consider the importance of professional development and learning opportunities for our caregivers. Did you know that the majority of early childhood caregivers have only a high school equivalent education? So the opportunity to provide research-based learning activities for sitters, nannies, au pairs, daycare workers was equally rich.

The data told the story of underutilized assets that could be – if properly empowered – optimized to create valuable learning opportunities. Every parent wants the best for their child. I saw an opportunity to provide a hungry audience with an easy to use solution. Most parents don't know how, don't have the time or bandwidth, or don't have access to means of providing the best. PU – and now this book – made sense from numerous perspectives.

The simple to do activities in *Parent Win* help you create a learning activity from everyday moments – whether it's in line at the store, folding laundry, making dinner, preparing for bedtime, making bath time fun and everything in between. I know that two of the most valuable things for a parent are your time and your sanity. :-) *Parent Win* activities are designed to help you save both while also keeping your kids engaged with high-quality interactions!

In addition to being grounded in a bevy of cross-disciplinary research, the "small acts" philosophy is also practical. And as you read in the pages that follow that is exactly what you will see: small acts that you can turn to throughout the years to do with your child to build very specific skills and, more broadly, craft a more enriching environment.

WHERE DID THIS COME FROM, ANYWAY?

In the history of *Parent Win*, 2009 was the most eventful. Not just because it was the period of time in which the concept was conceived. But because of the perfect storm of events that incepted the founding of what would eventually become *Parent Win*.

Illustrative of a small portion of that storm: I had completed a longitudinal ethnographic study of effective literacy training practices and I was developing ways for implementing and making the findings actionable. My first niece had recently been born, and as a family we were obsessing over Paityn's development.

My research and classroom experiences helped me develop a paradigm defined by small acts being performed repeatedly. With my sisters Kelley and Kassie (both of whom are education/developmental experts in their own right) we would text back and forth the latest research we had read about everything from in-utero language exposure as a child's first exposure to the rhythms of language or the role of babbling as a means of developing pre-language muscle controls or the role of pretend reading as early exposure to literacy concepts and so on.

Perhaps the most influential of the formative experiences at this time was my friendship with Charlize. Charlize, the single mother of a seven year old, and sole breadwinner of her household, made an indelible mark on my understanding of parenthood. By all accounts she was a great mother. She did everything she could to provide the best for her little girl. Charlize, however, was constantly stressed out about whether or not she was doing well enough. She was an incredible caregiver and a great mom. But no matter how well she did on a given day or throughout the weeks, the one thing that she needed more than anything else was support. A pat on the back, a hug, encouragement that, yes, you are doing great and your little one is going to be just fine.

These pats on the back were glaringly absent not just for Charlize, but for every mom and dad – including me! One of the research findings of our parent community, the majority of which were moms, showed that they felt these same feelings of isolation, insecurity and just plain not knowing whether they were providing the best for their child's early development. Years later, I am proud to say, of the several poignant research findings pertaining to the impact on *Parent Win* users, moms and dads reported feeling supported, less isolated, and more recognized for the tough job they have.

FORMAT OF THE BOOK

The format of the book is that each week consists of at least five activities. The activities are grouped by themes such as language development, fine motor skills, emotional bonding, etc. for you to do with your child. For the overwhelming majority of the activities you won't need to buy any supplies, toys, subscriptions or any other accouterment – though you certainly may enhance the activities by doing so. I also encourage you to be creative, ad lib and, most importantly, have fun!

Happy Learning!

Chris Drew, Ph.D.

PARENT'S NOTES

Advice from Our Readers

MONTH ZERO

Chris Drew, Ph.D.

SETTING REALISTIC EXPECTATIONS
ABOUT "BALANCE"

Jessica B. Mom to Connor and Baby Girl (on the way),
Walnut Creek, CA

When I was pregnant the first time I wish I had been given more real life advice, been told what it really is like to raise kids, work full time, maintain healthy relationships, etc. Reflecting back over the past two years with my first child and preparing to do it again with my second, the biggest thing that stands out in my mind is that elusive "balance" people always tell you to strive for. Since nobody told me, I want to take time to share one real insight that nobody shared with me.

In the first year I was working just to survive my adjustment to this new life. And during this transition, I can tell you, there is no such thing as "balance". Balance is a load of crap. It's as fictional as Princess Aurora sleeping 100 years or Ariel trading her tail for legs or Arthur yanking a sword from a giant, ancient stone.

I write this with a two year old pulling at my arm, another baby in my belly, a half-eaten plate of dinner on my lap, and an inbox with hundreds of unread messages. I question my sanity on a daily basis of adding another child to the mix, but then I look at my son and cannot believe how quickly he has grown into a full-fledged little boy complete with truck obsessions and mini tantrums.

We've gone through some lows: his scary birth, projectile vomit episodes, ear infections leading to ear tube surgery, injuries, you name it. We've also had many highs: when he first smiled at me, started crawling, walking, talking, giving the biggest hugs you could imagine, saying I love baby sis for the first time. Yes, typical baby things. But I learned the hard way that you cannot focus on or truly appreciate typical baby things when you are also trying to be that perfect, balanced mom - work full time, pump at work, maintain some sort of semblance of a marriage, friendships, family relationships, never mind sleep, exercise to lose the baby weight, eat, the list goes on.

What I've learned through all of this, especially the early days when I was still striving to be the textbook definition of balanced, was that you cannot be balanced at all; it simply doesn't work. In order to survive the lows and truly appreciate the highs, you MUST step out of balance. Our first few months at home, do I regret not spending more time with friends or working out? Sorry but no. I needed to learn how to be a mother to my son more than my friends or my skinny jeans needed me. Once I was back at work did I feel guilty leaving him at daycare? Of course I did, but I needed to learn how to be a functioning adult again and my son needed to learn how to be independent. When he had his ear tubes surgery do I even remember what I missed at work? No way! I remember comforting him. I just wish someone had told me early on to ditch my balance expectations at the door and focus on what is truly important in the present. It would have saved a lot of tears and stressful days trying to do it all.

~ Jessica B., Walnut Creek, CA

PARENT WIN

Essential Activities
To Nurture Smarter Kids

THE FIRST YEAR

MONTH

○ ALL THE TIME   MONTH ①

ACTIVITY 1

According to pediatrics professor Raylene Phillips, MD, "Mothers who hold their newborns skin to skin after birth have increased maternal behaviors, show more confidence in caring for their babies and breastfeed for longer durations."

Cuddle and make physical contact with your baby. It is a big part of the first month of bonding as a family - not just for mom and baby, but everybody in the family. This can be done while doing other activities with your baby: feeding, napping, singing, etc.

DEVELOPMENTAL FOCUS	RECOMMENDED RESOURCES
Family bonding	Bare skin

10-60 MINUTES   MONTH ①

ACTIVITY 2

Go for a walk outside. This is good for mom and baby. If it's cold you can walk around the mall. Head to a park, coffee shop, or friend's house for a destination. Or just walk around the block to get some fresh air and sunshine.

DEVELOPMENTAL FOCUS	RECOMMENDED RESOURCES
Mental well-being (for mom and dad!)	A destination within walking distance

_____

_____

_____

2-5 MINUTES   MONTH 1

ACTIVITY 3

Explain noises around you that you hear. Point in the direction of the noise. Describe the thing that made the noise. Be still and listen to see if the noise occurs again. "Shhh. Did you hear that? It was the clock on the mantle in front of us going 'tick tock tick tock'". Or, "Did you hear that? It's the hum of the dryer spinning really fast drying our clothes. It's coming from the other room. Let's see if it gets louder if we walk in that direction..." (Don't forget about all the senses - you can do this with your sense of smell, sight, touch. Taste will come later.)

DEVELOPMENTAL FOCUS	RECOMMENDED RESOURCES
Listening (auditory) skills	New or unique noises (which for your newborn is pretty much everything)

2-5 MINUTES   MONTH ①

ACTIVITY 4

Routines and predictability are one of the ways that your newborn begins to develop a sense of security in this new world of theirs. You can create routines by making games out of everyday (or even mundane!) activities, like singing the same song at bathtime. They will begin to associate the Rubber Ducky song with preparing for bath time (or Twinkle Twinkle Little Star with bedtime).

DEVELOPMENTAL FOCUS	RECOMMENDED RESOURCES
Emotional Awareness Family Bonding Trust Predictability	Your songbird voice or a set of activities (a routine) that you do the same way every time.

20 MINUTES   MONTH ①

ACTIVITY 5

Skin-to-skin contact is very important for your baby to feel calm and comfortable. Lay down with your baby on your chest or with her belly touching your belly while she is taking a nap. Take a nap with her or hang out and watch TV.

DEVELOPMENTAL
FOCUS

RECOMMENDED
RESOURCES

Family bonding

Baby, Mom, Dad

5-30 MINUTES   MONTH 1

ACTIVITY 6

Did you know that even while in the mother's womb you baby was learning your voice and picking up on language patterns? The simple act of talking to your child and talking with your child stimulates their brain. Have a conversation with your baby. Describe the food you're eating or the colors in the room where you're sitting or tell her a story about your high school prom!

DEVELOPMENTAL FOCUS

Vocabulary building
Conversational
turn-taking
Eye contact and social
engagement

RECOMMENDED RESOURCES

Your soothing, loving voice.

---

30 MINUTES   MONTH 1

ACTIVITY 7

According to brain scientist Lise Eliot, "there can be little doubt that the quality of children's language exposure also permanently shapes the structure and function of their linguistic brains." So in addition to doing "baby talk" with your child, have your child around while you're having adult conversations, too.

DEVELOPMENTAL FOCUS

Language skills
Vocabulary building
Conversational turn-taking
Eye contact and social engagement

RECOMMENDED RESOURCES

Friend or family member to have a fun, engaging conversation with.

_____
_____
_____

5-30 MINUTES   MONTH ①

ACTIVITY 8

While doing daily chores explain to your child what you're doing. Baby doesn't yet understand exactly what you're saying, but the exposure to language is very important. This is super easy. For example, describe to your baby: "I'm changing your diaper". "I'm going to get you dressed now". "I'm doing the dishes".

DEVELOPMENTAL FOCUS	RECOMMENDED RESOURCES
Narration skills Vocabulary building Conversational turn-taking Eye contact and social engagement	Your highly engaging, colorful, creative narration skills

5-30 MINUTES   MONTH 1

ACTIVITY 9

When talking to your child use facial expressions and hand gestures. For example, point to items you're describing, shrug your shoulders as you say "I don't know", etc. This is an important part of language for baby to learn, and it is fun for them to watch.

DEVELOPMENTAL FOCUS

Language skills
Body language skills
Vocabulary building
Listening skills

RECOMMENDED RESOURCES

A fun topic
Creative hand gestures
and body language

10 MINUTES   MONTH 1

ACTIVITY 10

Dad, in these early months baby will be spending a lot of time with mommy. Stay patient. Both mom and baby really need you during these early months. One thing you can do is pick a single activity that is just for you and baby. You could come up with a song that only you sing. Do a lil dance with baby each time you change diapers. Get into the habit of doing a special daddy-baby activity so you can create your special bond, too.

DEVELOPMENTAL   RECOMMENDED
FOCUS   RESOURCES

Daddy-Baby Bonding   Daddy and baby

_____

_____

_____

5-30 MINUTES   MONTH 1

ACTIVITY 11

Your baby will enjoy looking at more than just high contrast colors. He will enjoy looking at a wide variety of colors! Show him pictures in a book, point out the different colors of leaves on the trees, etc. Say the colors as you point.

DEVELOPMENTAL
FOCUS

RECOMMENDED
RESOURCES

Color identification

Picture books
Walk in the park
The outfit you're
wearing
Anything, anywhere
where you can point
out colors!

30 MINUTES–DAYS, WEEKS, MONTHS!　MONTH　1

ACTIVITY 12

Remember, for your baby to get used to more than one adult spending time with her it is important for her to build loving relationships with more than one person. Having your baby spend time with family and friends is important for lots of reasons.

DEVELOPMENTAL FOCUS	RECOMMENDED RESOURCES
Family bonding Socializing skills Learning to love and be loved	Family Friends Parent group

10 MINUTES;
4 HOURS PER DAY   MONTH 1

ACTIVITY 13

Keep having conversations with your baby. He won't be talking back quite yet, but he is listening to every word you say.

Bonus: For over three decades research has found, and research continues to reinforce, that the quantity and quality of words that a child is exposed to during the first 60 months of life directly impacts their success later in life.

DEVELOPMENTAL FOCUS	RECOMMENDED RESOURCES
Language Develop-ment	Family
Vocabulary building	Friends
Social skills	Moms groups
	Dads groups

_____

_____

_____

EVERYDAY!   MONTH **1**

ACTIVITY 14

Hey mom and dad, we wanted to take a second to tell you what an awesome job you're doing! Being a parent is one of the toughest jobs in the world and you're doing great at it!

DEVELOPMENTAL FOCUS	RECOMMENDED RESOURCES
Parenting confidence	Mirror

_____

_____

_____

10 MINUTES; ALL THE TIME

MONTH 1

ACTIVITY 15

Use different expressions in your voice when talking to your baby. Fluctuate your tone, volume, pitch, speed, etc. Speak really quickly with a high pitch as you express something exciting. Slow down your speech and volume to express something serious.

DEVELOPMENTAL FOCUS

RECOMMENDED RESOURCES

Language skills

Your voice

20 MINUTES   MONTH 1

ACTIVITY 16

Toys are important, but sheer number matters much less than variety. It's a good idea, therefore, to rotate different toys and play materials every week or so. An even better trick is to trade toys with friends or neighbors. Think creatively to find new ways to stimulate your child without breaking the bank on new toys!

Repurposing Creatively: Toys can be re-purposed during different phases (e.g. a tummy time play mat becomes infinitely more interesting to a crawling baby if you take off the hangie toys and put them on the floor).

DEVELOPMENTAL   RECOMMENDED
FOCUS   RESOURCES

Mommy and Daddy   Toys
Craftiness

2 MINUTES   MONTH **1**

ACTIVITY 17

The best way to sustain babies' interest is to show them new things. (Babies get bored, too, sometimes.) Try to offer variations on a theme. For example Itsy Bitsy Spider goes up the water spout. But switch it up sometimes: move their arms in different ways, or focus on different body parts, colors, shapes, or sounds. Encouraging children's attention, even very early in infancy, helps foster the persistence and motivation they need to master ever more difficult challenges.

DEVELOPMENTAL FOCUS	RECOMMENDED RESOURCES
Mommy and Daddy Creativeness	**Imagination**

5 MINUTES   MONTH 1

ACTIVITY 18

You've probably noticed that part of this week's theme centers around variety and creative approaches to keeping baby's attention. What is one of the ways you have been creative or introduced variety to your baby?

DEVELOPMENTAL
FOCUS

RECOMMENDED
RESOURCES

**Mommy and Daddy
Craftiness**

None

_____

_____

_____

10 MINUTES   MONTH   1

ACTIVITY 19

Read a picture book to your little one and use different voices for each character. She will love looking at the pictures and hearing different tones in your voice as you shift your voice for the different characters in the story. And don't forget to add the special effect sounds of creaking branches, flapping bird wings, or whatever may be going on in the pictures!

Bonus for Mom and Dad: If you ever give presentations at work, tell stories while getting your nails done, or deliver jokes while playing poker, reading time can be a great time to practice your public speaking skills. If you've ever noticed some of the best public speakers, they are skilled at softening their voice or pausing for dramatic effect. Speakers who keep your attention add inflections or increase the speed of their speech (or slow down) to create intensity and other emotions. Give it a try with your little one.

DEVELOPMENTAL FOCUS	RECOMMENDED RESOURCES
Pre-literacy and story telling	Books and fun voices

_____

_____

_____

30 MINUTES   MONTH 1

ACTIVITY 20

Keeping your baby healthy means being conscientious of your own health. It is just as important for mom and dad to stay healthy as it is for baby. If you can try to sneak in a nap, a quick jog, a few yoga poses, or a meditative shower, do so. Babies can pick up on our emotional states, including our stress. So be sure to create an outlet for yourself when you need it.

DEVELOPMENTAL
FOCUS

Mental health

RECOMMENDED
RESOURCES

Bed, shower, or
jogging shoes

_____

_____

_____

2 MINUTES   MONTH 1

ACTIVITY 21

These first few weeks are precious moments for bonding that you'll remember forever. Take time to watch your baby sleep. Create an eating ritual where you stroke your baby's hands or head as they nurse.

DEVELOPMENTAL FOCUS	RECOMMENDED RESOURCES
Family bonding	Calm moment

_____

_____

_____

10 MINUTES   MONTH 1

ACTIVITY 22

Singing is a very important thing for your child to hear. Each night if you sing a lullaby while you and your baby are relaxing, your baby will begin to associate that soothing emotion with the sound of your singing voice. You'll be able to sing to your baby to calm her down during times of high stress. You don't have to have the best voice to enjoy this activity with your child. And you don't have to sing just nursery rhymes. What's your favorite song? Sing it.

DEVELOPMENTAL FOCUS

Family bonding

RECOMMENDED RESOURCES

Your voice

_____

_____

_____

10 MINUTES   MONTH 1

ACTIVITY 23

To introduce your child to a variety of
music all it takes is to add some variety.
Turn on a different Pandora station and
read the descriptions of the music being
played. Get up and dance, bop your head,
snap your fingers, or glide on your toes
with your baby or your partner. Try out
classical music, modern rock, jazz, blues,
pop, hip-hop, whatever. You can use any
music genre you want. Have some fun
with it.

DEVELOPMENTAL   RECOMMENDED
FOCUS   RESOURCES

Music   Radio or smartphone

10 MINUTES   MONTH 1

ACTIVITY 25

When songs have lyrics that include body parts or objects that are in the room be sure to point them out to your child. "Head and shoulders, knees and toes, knees and toes..." If you're singing Patty Cake, Itsy Bitsy Spider, Hokey Pokey, etc. simply describe how you're clapping your hands, touching your finger tips, and so on. Point to each body part. This will help baby's receptive language skills.

DEVELOPMENTAL   RECOMMENDED
FOCUS   RESOURCES

Language   Songs

5 MINUTES   MONTH 1

ACTIVITY 26

Moving your child's arms and legs to the rhythm and beat of the music will help them learn about music. This is called kin-esthetic learning.

DEVELOPMENTAL FOCUS	RECOMMENDED RESOURCES
Motor skills and Kin-esthetic development	Baby's body

_____

_____

_____

5 MINUTES   MONTH ①

ACTIVITY 27

Mom and dad, you are still doing a great job! Listen to music that you enjoy. Get up and dance to it. Take a break and bust a move! This will help keep you happy and positive and feel like you have extra energy.

DEVELOPMENTAL FOCUS

Fun

RECOMMENDED RESOURCES

Music

Chris Drew, Ph.D.

PARENT'S NOTES
Advice from Our Readers
MONTH ONE

THE ALMOST HIKE

Tony K., Dad to Molly, Burlingame, CA

One of my favorite things in this world is hiking amongst the redwood trees of northern California. Trekking through the meandering trails of the coastal ranges near our home is my Om. Like caffeine to a coffee drinker, I've come to rely on and need this fresh air injection with some regularity. So it didn't take long – four weeks, actually – before I was able to convince the wife to bundle up the baby and head for the hills.

Of course bundling up the baby for what was our first outdoor mini-adventure entailed packing my 65 liter backpack to the brim with what seemed like the totality of every baby thing we had ever purchased: 100 diapers, 3 packs of wipes, 3 different hats, 2 fall sweatshirt, 1 winter jacket, booties, socks, blankets, Boba wrap, more socks (for her hands), Bob stroller, Ergo 360... you get the idea.

After packing, changing, and dressing everybody for an hour, then driving 45 minutes to Corte Madera Creek, our favorite hiking spot, we finally arrived at the trail head. Finally! My oasis. My retreat. I had been excited for selfish reasons (duh!). But I was also thrilled to be introducing my baby to one of my favorite pastimes. How fantastic would it be if she came to love the outdoors as much as her daddy?!

So we begin unpacking the car and loading up the backpack and strapping on the Ergo. We were off to the woods! ...well, sort of. We made it approximately 30 yards when she started to get a bit fussy. She decided she needed to eat. So out from the Ergo she came. After 6 or 7 minutes of eating we were ready to get going again.

But then she needed a diaper change.

After the diaper change, then she didn't want to go back into the Ergo.

She also found the Boba intolerable.

Then she needed a nap.

After 45 minutes of standing at the trail head, frustrated and dejected, I decided the best course of action would be to head back home so she could sleep in her own bed.

Such is my life now. After three and a half decades of doing pretty much whatever I wanted to do when I wanted to do it, I now have a dictator in my life that puts the kibosh on pretty much anything I find enjoyable: live sporting events, hikes, concerts, dining out, comedy clubs, lazy afternoons at a café. Accepting this fact has been the hardest adjustment. At the peril of going mad, luckily, it's an adjustment that I'm finally starting to accept.

~ Tony K., Burlingame, CA

PARENT WIN

*Essential Activities
To Nurture Smarter Kids*

THE FIRST YEAR

MONTH

10 MINUTES   MONTH 2

ACTIVITY 1

"Speech is without a doubt the most important form of stimulation a baby receives. When parents talk to their babies, they are activating hearing, social, emotional, and linguistic centers of the brain all at once, but their influence on language development is especially profound."

~ Lise Eliot, Ph.D.

This nugget from Professor Eliot highlights in a nutshell the importance of simply talking to your baby. The conversation topics can be about anything you want or nothing at all. The benefits of interacting with your baby activate so many parts of her brain. So chat it up!

DEVELOPMENTAL FOCUS	RECOMMENDED RESOURCES
Language Development	Conversation topics

10 MINUTES   MONTH ②

ACTIVITY 2

To help your baby with her sleeping habits in the future, let her fall asleep with noise in the background: music, white noise, people talking, etc. This will help her as she gets older to be able to fall asleep easier in more diverse circumstances. And it will also help you and your partner keep your sanity!

DEVELOPMENTAL FOCUS	RECOMMENDED RESOURCES
Sanity check for Mom and Dad	Noise and flexibility

_____

_____

_____

◯ 0 MINUTES　　　　　MONTH ②

ACTIVITY 3

During this time your baby is too young to begin a routine of sleeping and eating. Feed her when she is hungry and let her sleep when she is sleepy. She will sleep about 20 hours per day at this time.

DEVELOPMENTAL
FOCUS

Sleeping, Eating, Growing

RECOMMENDED
RESOURCES

Patience

_____

_____

_____

10 MINUTES   MONTH 2

ACTIVITY 4

Dad, what's your special daddy-baby bonding activity for this month? If baby is starting to take a bottle, maybe you could be the one who always makes the bottle. Do you have a favorite book? Make a rap song or country song out of it. Sing the book like an opera to baby. Practice your story telling by telling and retelling your favorite sports playoff memory with the voice of an announcer. This is your special thing with baby for the month. Keep doing it, Dad!

DEVELOPMENTAL
FOCUS

Daddy-Baby Bonding

RECOMMENDED
RESOURCES

Daddy and baby

10 MINUTES   MONTH 2

ACTIVITY 5

When your baby is awake, talk to her, touch her skin, take a walk around the house with her. Explain to her what each room is. She will look around and feel more comfortable with where she is.

DEVELOPMENTAL
FOCUS

Trust

RECOMMENDED
RESOURCES

Conversation

60 MINUTES   MONTH (2)

ACTIVITY 6

Joining parent groups or going to community events is a fun way of building a support network and getting out and about. Get online and look up reading times at your local library. Search for sign language classes at your local hospital, do a Google search for mommy groups or daddy daycares, or music meet ups, etc. Depending on your community there are likely lots opportunities for you to connect with other families and get involved in groups that will be a blast for you and your baby.

DEVELOPMENTAL FOCUS	RECOMMENDED RESOURCES
Social Skills	Transportation to the group meeting

30 MINUTES   MONTH ②

ACTIVITY 7

If you're baby has colic you need to do a few things: Find a way to get a break from your baby for at least an hour. Take a shower with some music playing. Make a schedule of getting out of the house at least once a day. Get a spoon and a tub of ice cream to treat your self. Rely on someone to confide in and vent to.

Our baby had colic and we spent six weeks with a baby who would scream in our face no matter what we did. Whether we changed her, fed her, swaddled her, sang to her, rocked her, drove her around... it didn't matter. She cried for six hours a day. We took her to the doctor numerous times. "Your baby has colic. She'll grow out of it." Eventually she did. But those were difficult weeks.

DEVELOPMENTAL FOCUS	RECOMMENDED RESOURCES
Mommy and Daddy Mental and Emotional Health	**A break**

_____

_____

_____

10 MINUTES   MONTH 2

ACTIVITY 8

Babies like to focus on colors with high contrast: black, red, and white for example. A good neighborhood bookstore, mommy group, library reading time, etc. will be able to recommend age appropriate books for your newborn. Remember, your baby cannot see very far at this stage, so bring pictures closer to her and don't worry if she's not responding or focusing just yet.

DEVELOPMENTAL FOCUS	RECOMMENDED RESOURCES
Pre-literacy	Books and fun voices

_____

_____

_____

5 MINUTES   MONTH 2

ACTIVITY 9

It's not too early to begin tummy time! This will help build your baby's neck muscles to help get better control of her head and to begin the process of preparing for sitting up.

DEVELOPMENTAL FOCUS	RECOMMENDED RESOURCES
Coordination and muscle building	Clean surface to lay on

5 MINUTES   MONTH 2

ACTIVITY 10

Let your baby fall asleep in more places than just her crib. Let her sleep on your chest, in the pack-and-play, in her car seat (if she is already asleep in it), in your arms. Just be sure you are sitting in a safe place where baby won't be at risk of falling or you rolling over onto her as you slumber.

DEVELOPMENTAL FOCUS	RECOMMENDED RESOURCES
Flexibility	Sleepy baby

_____

_____

_____

7 MINUTES   MONTH 2

ACTIVITY 11

It's important for your baby (and you!) to get fresh air. If it's nice outside, take your baby on a ride in her stroller. Wrap her in a blanket and stroll around your block. Point out the swaying trees, the gliding birds, the cars zooming past, or whatever other actions you can narrate as you walk.

DEVELOPMENTAL FOCUS	RECOMMENDED RESOURCES
Language Development	Safe sidewalk or outdoor path

10 MINUTES   MONTH 2

ACTIVITY 12

Talk to your baby about all of the noises she will hear outside (birds chirping, squirrels playing with leaves, etc.). We learn through repetition. And as you know by now, the more diverse vocabulary and other language features your baby hears the more she is going to develop cognitively. As well, your baby will continue to become more familiar with your voice, which will comfort her in times of fussiness.

DEVELOPMENTAL FOCUS	RECOMMENDED RESOURCES
Language	**Your voice**

Chris Drew, Ph.D.

10 MINUTES   MONTH 2

ACTIVITY 13

Your baby will go through various phases, such as an attachment phase where he only wants to be held by mommy or daddy. Before that phase arrives, let your baby get used to having other people hold him. If he is only held by one person all the time, he will get overly attached and inconsolable when he want his mommy or daddy.

DEVELOPMENTAL FOCUS

Trust

RECOMMENDED RESOURCES

Loved ones

10 MINUTES   MONTH 2

ACTIVITY 14

Play music throughout your house. Play different types of music! Let your baby enjoy different songs that you love.

DEVELOPMENTAL FOCUS	RECOMMENDED RESOURCES
Pre-literacy	Books and fun voices

_____

_____

_____

⏱ 5 MINUTES   MONTH ②

ACTIVITY 15

Caring for a newborn can sometimes be frustrating and emotionally taxing. If you get frustrated it's okay to take a timeout for yourself. Place your baby in a safe place, like her crib. Take deep breaths, go into another room, take a shower, do some jumping jacks, or do some other activity that gives you respite. It's okay if your baby is crying, you can come back to tend to your baby once you've calmed down.

DEVELOPMENTAL FOCUS

Calm

RECOMMENDED RESOURCES

Patience

_____
_____
_____

30 MINUTES   MONTH 2

ACTIVITY 16

Be sure you make time for yourself. Your baby is brand new. It's important to sleep when she is sleeping. When she is awake, take 30 minutes to go read a book, shop, take a walk, etc.

DEVELOPMENTAL
FOCUS

Relaxation

RECOMMENDED
RESOURCES

Relaxing room

_____

_____

_____

🕐 3 MINUTES   MONTH ②

ACTIVITY 17

When you are dressing your baby, remember not to bundle the little one too much. She only needs one layer more than you do to stay warm.

DEVELOPMENTAL FOCUS	RECOMMENDED RESOURCES
Temperature regulation	Weather–appropriate layers

_____

_____

_____

⏲ 2 MINUTES   MONTH ②

ACTIVITY 18

If you haven't started your baby sleeping in her crib yet, let her get more comfortable with her crib by letting her take naps in it. This will help the transition from bassinet, for example, to her crib.

DEVELOPMENTAL
FOCUS

Trust and Comfort

RECOMMENDED
RESOURCES

Crib

_____

_____

_____

10 MINUTES   MONTH 2

ACTIVITY 19

Your child is already learning how to express himself. Your baby uses cries to communicate his wants and needs and may cry, coo or grunt based on different emotions. Listen close. Have you learned what some of the new cries mean?

DEVELOPMENTAL FOCUS

RECOMMENDED RESOURCES

Pre-literacy

Books and fun voices

2 MINUTES   MONTH 2

ACTIVITY 20

Validate your child's cries or attempts at communication by commenting "Oh your hungry? Okay, let's get you a bottle!" "Oh you have a wet diaper. Momma/Daddy is going to change it." Cries, grunts, coos are the only way your baby has of communicating. By giving conversational responses to these communicative cries you're starting to teach your child important language skills like turn-taking, social skills, and conversational conventions.

DEVELOPMENTAL FOCUS	RECOMMENDED RESOURCES
Language Development	Situational awareness (and a small bit of guessing)

_____

_____

_____

7 MINUTES   MONTH 2

ACTIVITY 21

When completing daily activities be sure you talk your baby through the actions you are performing. This exposes them to the rhythms of conversation and to rich vocabulary. For example, while changing baby's diapers say "Let's take this dirty diaper off and toss it in the trash receptacle. Now I'll wipe your bottom clean." It can be a fun challenge for you and your partner to come up with new vocabulary words each day.

DEVELOPMENTAL FOCUS

RECOMMENDED RESOURCES

Language (Vocabulary building)

Expanded vocabulary/ Thesaurus

2 MINUTES   MONTH 2

ACTIVITY 22

In the beginning your baby can be very demanding. Crying and cooing are baby's way of communicating. Talking back to them in soothing voices can help calm and reassure your baby. And remember, moms and dads across the realm get frustrated with their cute lil bundles of "joy", too. That's normal.

DEVELOPMENTAL   RECOMMENDED
FOCUS   RESOURCES

Language Develop-   Conversations
ment

_____

_____

_____

1 MINUTES   MONTH 2

ACTIVITY 23

Rub your babies back or feet or legs. Give her hugs and kisses. You want your little one to get used to being loved, talked to, and touched with care. This continues to build your bonds of love and trust.

DEVELOPMENTAL
FOCUS

Love and Trust

RECOMMENDED
RESOURCES

Hugs and Kisses

PARENT'S NOTES
Advice from Our Readers
MONTH TWO

ANXIETY: AM I DOING THIS RIGHT?

Laura B., Mom to Lilly, Redwood City, CA

Maybe it's because I always strove to be a "star student" as a kid. Or maybe it's because I'm a teacher as an adult. Or maybe, as a major Type A person, this is simply my destiny when approaching new experiences. But the question "What is the *right* way to [fill in the blank]?" hounded me during all my diligent pre-natal reading about having a baby and through every action and decision I was making after giving birth. Looking back, it feels like I was preparing for a test – How to have and raise a baby – and that there was some answer key that others (other parents, other grandparents, siblings, and even strangers) would be using to check my work on a daily basis.

Inevitably, I quite often felt lost, confused, and overwhelmed by a seemingly infinite number of answer choices for any given topic and flailing around blindly to figure out the "right" answer. What are the *right* baby items to register for? What is the *right* birth plan? What is the *right* way to get my child to sleep? What is the *right* way to get my child to like her car seat? I found myself attempting some version of "cheating" at this imaginary test, watching other moms love and care for their child and assuming everything they choose to do must be "right;" therefore, I must choose that, too.

Eventually, I realized that this attitude was good at only one thing – not at achieving the sought-after A+ on being a mom I was apparently aiming for but rather setting me up for a whole lot of feelings of anxiety and inadequacy. I know, now, that there is no one right answer; I know that there are many ways to approach having and raising a baby and that whatever works for my child and my family one day will likely not work another day. I also appreciate the value of seeing others parent, not to feel like my choices have been wrong but to feel grateful to be exposed to other different yet equally valuable ways of doing things.

~ Laura B., Redwood City, CA

PARENT WIN

Essential Activities
To Nurture Smarter Kids

THE FIRST YEAR

MONTH

◯ 0 MINUTES   MONTH ③

ACTIVITY 1

By month 3 you will see your baby become even more interactive. This will be more rewarding for you as a parent. It will show that your efforts of having conversations with, singing to and working with your baby is paying off.

DEVELOPMENTAL FOCUS	RECOMMENDED RESOURCES
Pre-literacy	Time to enjoy

_____

_____

_____

🕐 10 MINUTES   MONTH ③

ACTIVITY 2

While supporting baby, put her in a sitting position. Put her on her bottom in between your legs and play with a toy or read a book. This will work on developing balance, and as you practice more sitting time she will become more independent with sitting skills. However, don't leave her by herself; she's still not quite strong enough to sit unsupervised.

DEVELOPMENTAL FOCUS

Balance and coordination

RECOMMENDED RESOURCES

Toy or book

_____

_____

_____

5 MINUTES   MONTH 3

ACTIVITY 3

Baby's eye muscles and eyesight is still developing. This includes being able to track movement quickly. You can help build this skill and the muscle movements by holding up baby's favorite toy and slowly moving it around for her to track. High contrast colors (e.g. black and white; white and red) on the page of a book can work too. From about three or four feet away, move them up, down, left, right, in a circle. Don't go too fast!

DEVELOPMENTAL   RECOMMENDED
FOCUS   RESOURCES

Tracking   Favorite toy

_____
_____
_____

3-5 MINUTES   MONTH 3

ACTIVITY 4

About this time your baby will start to hold his head up during tummy time. So during tummy time lay out in front of baby books with simple pictures and bright colors. This will help keep baby's attention and keep him from getting bored. Of course, keep in mind that he probably won't be doing tummy time for an extended period. Maybe only 3-5 minutes at this point.

DEVELOPMENTAL FOCUS	RECOMMENDED RESOURCES
Strength	Books or toys

_____

_____

_____

5 MINUTES   MONTH 3

ACTIVITY 5

Dad, remember, we are no match for the boob. Mom and baby will probably continue to have a closer bond. It's only natural. And even though you may be feeling left out, mom needs your support more than ever. Buy mommy some flowers. You'll be her hero! Then set an example for baby by telling baby all about what a gentleman you are. For your lil prince this is how he should expect to treat a lady later in life. For your lil princess this is how she should expect to be treated when she grows. Keep up the good example, Dad! You're making a huge impact through your strength, patience, and good examples. We learn more by the repetitious actions we are surrounded by than by the words people say to us.

DEVELOPMENTAL FOCUS	RECOMMENDED RESOURCES
Daddy–Baby Bonding	Daddy and baby

_____

_____

_____

◯ 0 MINUTES   MONTH ③

ACTIVITY 6

Developmental milestones are general targets. Some babies will achieve certain milestones sooner and achieve other milestones later than others. For example, one of my nieces didn't start walking until after she was 20 months old. However, she started talking and saying fully formed words at 9 months. Every child is different. If you have any concerns talk to your doctor.

DEVELOPMENTAL FOCUS

General development

RECOMMENDED RESOURCES

Patience and awareness

_____

_____

_____

40 MINUTES A DAY   MONTH 3

ACTIVITY 7

According to research in Child Development, "the most obvious influence over children's language development turned out to be the mere amount of parents' talking; children whose parents addressed or responded to them more in early life had larger, faster-growing vocabularies and scored higher on IQ tests later in life than children whose parents spoke fewer words to them overall."

DEVELOPMENTAL FOCUS	RECOMMENDED RESOURCES
Language	Conversations

5 MINUTES   MONTH 3

ACTIVITY 8

Have playtime in front of a mirror. Point, wave, smile, giggle, talk, and sing. At this age baby won't recognize that it is a reflection of him self. But that's not the point. Your baby is watching your mouth movements as you talk. He will be seeing the "other baby" making movements and smiling and wiggling around. It is a good social and emotional skills building activity for the whole family.

DEVELOPMENTAL FOCUS	RECOMMENDED RESOURCES
Bonding and Social Skills	Bathroom or bedroom mirror

○ 0 MINUTES   MONTH ③

ACTIVITY 9

Fine motor skills such as manipulating utensils with fingers, gross motor skills such as balance, and language skills all develop during the critical first year of life. It is important to address all of these skills. But don't be alarmed if one skill develops faster or slower than one of these other skills.

DEVELOPMENTAL FOCUS	RECOMMENDED RESOURCES
Development	Patience and awareness

_____

_____

_____

10 MINUTES   MONTH 3

ACTIVITY 10

What are some ways you can work on gross motor skills? Continue working on sitting upright and sitting independently. The Bumbo Floor Seat is a parent favorite for independent sitting. Can your baby sit upright? Have her join you when you eat and include her in your conversations.

DEVELOPMENTAL
FOCUS

Strength, balance,
socializing

RECOMMENDED
RESOURCES

Bumbo

_____

_____

_____

ACTIVITY 11

A fine motor skill that you can work on with your baby is tracking – the process of following an object, voice or movement with your eyes. While baby is sitting, roll a ball back and forth with her. Watch as her eyes follow the ball.

DEVELOPMENTAL
FOCUS

RECOMMENDED
RESOURCES

Fine motor skills

Ball

60 MINUTES   MONTH 3

ACTIVITY 12

After you put baby to bed, take a few moments to be still and have some alone time or some alone time with your partner. Close your eyes, breath deeply and listen to soothing music. You deserve it!

DEVELOPMENTAL
FOCUS

RECOMMENDED
RESOURCES

Relaxation

Candles and soft
music

_____

_____

_____

◑ 30 MINUTES   MONTH ③

ACTIVITY 13

The live voices of mom, dad, family and friends are much better for baby than TV or cartoon voices. Limit exposure to TV or radio by turning off your TV for a while. Let baby participate in a conversation by watching and listening to the rhythms of family conversation.

DEVELOPMENTAL
FOCUS

RECOMMENDED
RESOURCES

Language and Social
skills

Family conversation

_____
_____
_____

10 MINUTES   MONTH 3

ACTIVITY 14

Literacy skills start at a very young age. It is important to start reading to your child very early and very often. Reading time before bed is a great way to establish a routine. Healthy routines are important for your baby! The best of both worlds: developing pre-literacy skills and a calming before bed activity to wind down the day.

DEVELOPMENTAL FOCUS

Pre-literacy

RECOMMENDED RESOURCES

Books

10 MINUTES   MONTH 3

ACTIVITY 15

It is important to choose age-appropriate books, books with simple pictures and high contrasting colors. Red, black and white are perfect contrasting colors for this stage. Share a picture with us: what is your favorite book to read with your baby?

DEVELOPMENTAL
FOCUS

Pre-literacy

RECOMMENDED
RESOURCES

Books

_____

_____

_____

10 MINUTES   MONTH 3

ACTIVITY 16

Some books at this age have very few words (or even no words) on each page. Even if there's only one word on each page, take the time to describe to your child each image you see on the page. Explaining and discussing the pictures expands your child's language exposure.

DEVELOPMENTAL
FOCUS

Pre-literacy and
Vocabulary Skills

RECOMMENDED
RESOURCES

Book with images

5 MINUTES   MONTH 3

ACTIVITY 17

Be sure to hold the book appropriately and turn the pages from the right side. These simple actions are part of developing early literacy skills. It's simple, and we grown ups take it for granted, but these book thingies are still new to baby!

DEVELOPMENTAL FOCUS	RECOMMENDED RESOURCES
Pre-literacy	Book

15 MINUTES   MONTH ③

ACTIVITY 18

If you're feeling frustrated or overwhelmed it's okay to put baby in their room or in their crib for a few minutes and take some time to get a breath of fresh air. Be sure to make sure baby is safe before you leave her alone.

DEVELOPMENTAL FOCUS	RECOMMENDED RESOURCES
Calm for mom and dad	Fresh air

_____

_____

_____

🕐 10 MINUTES   MONTH ③

ACTIVITY 19

While preparing a meal have your child sit in the bouncer and watch you. Describe to him what you are doing and why. You may not be a chef yet but he will enjoy the entertainment.

DEVELOPMENTAL FOCUS

RECOMMENDED RESOURCES

Language Development

Whatever is for lunch or dinner

5 MINUTES   MONTH 3

ACTIVITY 20

While folding the laundry name the articles of clothing that you are folding and the color of the clothes. Include a couple games of peek-a-boo to add to the fun!

DEVELOPMENTAL
FOCUS

RECOMMENDED
RESOURCES

Vocabulary building
and Color skills

Clean laundry – or
clean enough laundry
;-)

_____

_____

_____

7 MINUTES   MONTH 3

ACTIVITY 21

While in the bathtub sing the head and shoulders, knees and toes song while touching each body part. Brightly colored bath toys are also fun to look at. Identify the colors for your child.

DEVELOPMENTAL FOCUS	RECOMMENDED RESOURCES
Gross Motor Skills	Bathtub and your singing voice

_____

_____

_____

60 MINUTES   MONTH 3

ACTIVITY 22

By this age your baby should be sleeping for longer stretches of time. Hopefully you're able to get more tasks done or catch up on some rest. Take a bath or treat yourself to your favorite guilty pleasure. You have earned it.

DEVELOPMENTAL FOCUS	RECOMMENDED RESOURCES
Mommy and Daddy sanity	Permission for yourself to enjoy a guilty pleasure

INFINITE MINUTES   MONTH 3
(You're a parent now;
diligence and concern
will last forever!)

ACTIVITY 23

Many of the natural reflexes you hear from your baby at meal time, such as coughing or belching, are all used to prevent choking while eating. This may even happen while nursing or taking a bottle. Don't be alarmed, but remain diligent and attentive during mealtime – especially in a few months when your baby starts nibbling on solids.

DEVELOPMENTAL   RECOMMENDED
FOCUS   RESOURCES

Eating skills   Parental diligence

PARENT'S NOTES
Advice from Our Readers
MONTH THREE

COLIC

Karin P., Mom to Oriana, San Francisco, CA

The things no one says out loud: You love, but you do not like your baby. You cry, a lot. Not as much as your baby obviously, but still noteworthy. Other people drive you insane with unwelcomed advice with suggestions like: gas causes colic; letting her cry it out works; you are holding her wrong; and on and on. You name it, we've heard it.

As mom to a colicky baby you will try ANYTHING. Someone in my mom's group used a Windy (basically a straw you put up your baby's butt to relieve gas), I started my daughter in swim lessons at 2 months just to have 30 minutes when she wasn't crying. I gave her gripe water, which I knew in my heart didn't work, but at least she wasn't crying (or sucking on my very sore boobs) for the 20 minutes I was giving it to her.

Colic is a word made up by doctors that's code for "we have no idea why your baby cries but contrary to every fiber in your body telling you otherwise, we don't think anything is physically wrong with her". EVERY-

Chris Drew, Ph.D.

ONE thinks their baby has colic - oh your baby cries an hour a day and is fussy between the hours of 5 and 10? News flash: they are just being a normal baby. My baby screams in my face inconsolably no less than 3 hours every day and some days it's 9!

~ Karin P., San Francisco, CA

PARENT WIN

Essential Activities
To Nurture Smarter Kids

THE FIRST YEAR

MONTH

20 MINUTES   MONTH 4

ACTIVITY 1

Sign language can be taught as early as right after birth. But it will take a while before baby is able to use signs to communicate with you. If you want to teach signs to your baby, it is important to start by signing with your partner for everyday things around the house. Baby will pick up on and imitate everything that you do.

DEVELOPMENTAL FOCUS

RECOMMENDED RESOURCES

Language Development

Gestures and sign language

_____

_____

_____

ACTIVITY 2

Dad, what's your special daddy-baby bonding routine for this month? Maybe it's poking your nose outside each day or night to find the moon. Maybe it's lining up your favorite BBQ sauces in a row and smelling and describing the flavors each Saturday. You could create a series of bedtime stories based on your best road trips ever (be sure to leave out any R-rated details ;-). Baby probably won't be able to find the moon, she may not eat the BBQ sauce yet, and she won't get the humor in your funny road trip stories, but that's okay. You're exposing her to diverse language, experiences, and forging a special bond. Keep up the great work, Dad!

DEVELOPMENTAL FOCUS

Daddy–Baby Bonding

RECOMMENDED RESOURCES

Daddy and baby

1 MINUTE   MONTH 4

ACTIVITY 3

Experts say it's never too early to start teaching sign language. Research shows that learning sign language before speech manifests has measurable positive impacts on language development. There are easy signs to teach that correspond to eating. The sign for "eat" is created by putting all of your fingers on your thumb and touching your bottom lip. Show baby how to do the sign and practice each time you eat. Repetition is key!

DEVELOPMENTAL FOCUS

RECOMMENDED RESOURCES

Language Development

Your hands (and remembering to do it each time you eat!)

🕐 1 MINUTE   MONTH ④

ACTIVITY 4

The sign for "all done" is represented by holding both hands in the air and shaking flicking them forward like you're (rudely) flipping food from your imaginary plate. Be sure to say "all done" out loud while doing the sign. It will be a few months before baby can do this gesture too. But in time baby will be able to tell you when she's all done eating. A great free app to see a rich library of sign language signs is called "Spread the Sign."

DEVELOPMENTAL FOCUS	RECOMMENDED RESOURCES
Language Development	Your hands

_____

_____

_____

1 MINUTE   MONTH 4

ACTIVITY 5

The sign for "more" is represented by put-ting your fingers to your thumb on each of your hands. Now tap together the finger-tips and thumb tips on each hand. Be sure to say "more" out loud as you tap. Don't expect your baby to be doing this in the days ahead. It's not until her fine motor skills start kicking in that she will be able to imitate this gesture. But in time, baby will be able to respond when you ask if she wants "more" or if he is "all done."

DEVELOPMENTAL FOCUS	RECOMMENDED RESOURCES
Language Develop-ment	**Your hands**

_____

_____

_____

1 MINUTE   MONTH 4

ACTIVITY 6

The sign for "milk" is represented by squeezing your fingers into your palm. Imagine the act of squeezing the utter of a cow to get milk. That's where the sign comes from! It may take awhile for baby to catch on and start using these signs. Be patient and keep repeating the signs. She'll catch on soon. Her brain is still absorbing it all.

DEVELOPMENTAL FOCUS

RECOMMENDED RESOURCES

Language Development

Your hands

20 MINUTES   MONTH 4

ACTIVITY 7

Start your week off by calling one of your friends who is a parent and give them an encouraging word. Sometimes doing something kind for another person can rejuvenate your spirits and make you feel better about yourself!

DEVELOPMENTAL
FOCUS

RECOMMENDED
RESOURCES

Mom and Dad's sanity

Phone and no reason at all to call a friend

⏱ 1 MINUTE   MONTH 4

ACTIVITY 8

Your baby is beginning to hold on to objects and put them in her mouth. So be on the lookout for choking hazards. When it comes to food, though, as your baby is tasting the object take time to describe the temperature, texture, color, etc. This is a great way to build vocabulary. For example, the banana is lukewarm, yellow, sticky, squishy, and delicious!

DEVELOPMENTAL FOCUS	RECOMMENDED RESOURCES
Vocabulary building	Food and your creative descriptions

_____

_____

_____

3 MINUTES   MONTH 4

ACTIVITY 9

Around this age baby may begin teething. Along with this your baby will drool more. Having a cool chewy toy will be helpful for the pain. Be careful, and don't give baby something that is too cold or frozen solid, though.

DEVELOPMENTAL
FOCUS

RECOMMENDED
RESOURCES

General development

Cool chew toy (and a bib for all the drool)

_____

_____

_____

25 MINUTES   **MONTH** 4

ACTIVITY 10

Whether or not your baby is starting baby food at this point in time it is important to include him at meal times even if he is unable to have the food you are having. Turn off the TV. Put away the phones. Have family conversation, and begin introducing your baby to dinnertime routines. He's part of the family, too, ya know!

DEVELOPMENTAL FOCUS

RECOMMENDED RESOURCES

Social skills

Dinner table and dinner conversation

20 MINUTES   MONTH 4

ACTIVITY 11

As you sit around the dinner table have a conversation with your loved ones. It is important for your baby to hear the flow of conversations. You may even want to ask baby some questions. Be sure to pause and listen to baby as she responds! :-)

DEVELOPMENTAL
FOCUS

RECOMMENDED
RESOURCES

Social Skills and Language Development

Family dinner conversation

60 MINUTES   MONTH 4

ACTIVITY 12

At this age many people may avoid going out to dinner or doing other social things with baby. It is important for baby to be involved in events like dinner or shopping or going to games so baby can learn expected behavior in social situations. Plus, going out with friends will help you keep your sanity!

DEVELOPMENTAL FOCUS	RECOMMENDED RESOURCES
Social skills	Social environments

_____

_____

_____

12 MINUTES   MONTH 4

ACTIVITY 13

At this age most babies are enjoying their bath times. Bath time is a good time to introduce new vocabulary: names of body parts, water temperature, colors of toys, texture of the wash rag and soap, and so on. "This water is scalding." "The water is too chilly." "The soap is slippery and makes your skin smooth." "The wash rag is scratchy and exfoliating." You get the idea. Get creative!

DEVELOPMENTAL FOCUS	RECOMMENDED RESOURCES
Language and Vocabulary development	Bath tub, soap, rag, toys, etc.

INFINITE MINUTES   MONTH 4
(Will this ever go away?
According to experienced
grandmas across the land...
No, it won't.)

ACTIVITY 14

When giving baths never leave your baby unattended. Even in an infant's tub with only an inch or two of liquid, water is a very dangerous thing. Be vigilant and be careful.

DEVELOPMENTAL
FOCUS

Parental awareness
and diligence

RECOMMENDED
RESOURCES

Love for your baby

30 MINUTES   MONTH 4

ACTIVITY 16

If baby is not yet sleeping through the night it will be important to create a routine. Babies learn best when they feel safe and have predictable and calm environments. What is something you do to create a routine? If you're unsure, call a friend or family member. But also keep in mind, if you have a Saul Alinsky type of resistant baby, it's not your fault. Could be that your baby is just super strong-willed. Try to be patient with her personality!

DEVELOPMENTAL FOCUS	RECOMMENDED RESOURCES
Trust and Expectation setting	Regular routine

_____

_____

_____

20 MINUTES   MONTH 4

ACTIVITY 16

Things to include in your bedtime routine include: final change of diaper, getting into pajamas, rocking with a song or book, bedtime prayer, night-time lullaby, turning on white noise machine, etc. Whatever your final few things are, do them and then go to bed. Same goes for you, too, mom and dad! What do you do to unwind for a good night's rest?

DEVELOPMENTAL FOCUS

RECOMMENDED RESOURCES

Trust, Routine, Habit formation

Routine

_____

_____

_____

1 MINUTE   MONTH 4

ACTIVITY 17

As you think of your bedtime routine it is important to remember for safety to keep everything out of your baby's crib. No blankets, toys or other objects should be in the crib with your baby at this point.

DEVELOPMENTAL FOCUS

Diligence

RECOMMENDED RESOURCES

Nothing

_____

_____

_____

ACTIVITY 18

Your baby may be laughing at some of the silly things that occur now. She may be showing off her first smiles. As a parent it is reinforcing to be able to entertain your baby and get feedback. Take pictures. Relish these moments. Your baby loves you and is showing you her affection! Lap it up!

DEVELOPMENTAL FOCUS	RECOMMENDED RESOURCES
Emotional awareness	Awareness of your babies expressions

_____

_____

_____

2 MINUTES   MONTH **4**

ACTIVITY 19

By now your baby will be able to follow a moving object with his eyes (tracking). As you are completing dinner or while doing chores try to continue to talk as you move around the room and have your child's eyes follow you. You may need to speak up. Don't get frustrated if it takes time for this developmental milestone to manifest. Every baby works on her own sweet timeline.

DEVELOPMENTAL FOCUS	RECOMMENDED RESOURCES
Auditory awareness	**Your voice**

_____

_____

_____

⏱ 1 MINUTE   MONTH ④

ACTIVITY 20

By this age your baby will know your voice. Try calling your baby by her name so she continues to learn it. Use your baby's name in conversation and while talking to her.

DEVELOPMENTAL
FOCUS

RECOMMENDED
RESOURCES

Auditory awareness

Your voice

---

40 MINUTES   MONTH ④

ACTIVITY 21

By now your baby may be able to roll over. It won't be long before he starts to crawl. Now is a good time to ensure your house is baby proofed. A good strategy is to crawl around just like your baby and look for things that he will see as he becomes mobile.

DEVELOPMENTAL
FOCUS

Gross motor skills

RECOMMENDED
RESOURCES

Creative perspective

_____

_____

_____

PARENT'S NOTES
Advice from Our Readers
MONTH FOUR

NO SUCH THING AS "THANK YOU" AT 3:00AM

John A., Dad to Alexa, Phoenix, AZ

"I'll get her."
"No no. I'll get her. You make bottle."
Three minutes later: "Here." (as I reach through the darkness to shove the bottle into my wife's hand).

That's it. 12 words. That's how we roll at 3:00 a.m. When you're awakened from a peaceful, restful slumber to the sounds of your screaming offspring there are no pleasantries. There's no such thing as "Would you mind doing X for me?" "Thank you, dear." "I appreciate that." Nope. Efficiency directed by the most Spartan formations and commands is all that's needed and, frankly, all I have energy enough to sputter from my tongue. Whatever is the quickest route for my head to get back into the warm, cozy indentation of my pillow, that's the motor movements I'm making. Not a single lip flicker more.

I do, in fact, love you, dear. And I'm sure that in 3 hours when we get our wake up call for the day that I will appreciate you again. But right now, no "thank you's", no "I love you's." That's superfluous energy spent at this most fragile period of my non-sleeping state.

I promise I'll make up for it with a shoulder rub on Friday night.

~ John A., Phoenix, AZ

MONTH

2 MINUTES   MONTH 5

ACTIVITY 1

This month your baby is staying awake for longer periods of time. You will see more smiles and giggles, and baby will continue to become more active, more mobile and will know his name even better. Does your baby look at you when you call his name? He should start to be able to identify a sound and track it by looking in the sound.

DEVELOPMENTAL
FOCUS

Social awareness

RECOMMENDED
RESOURCES

Your voice

_____

_____

_____

5 MINUTES   MONTH 5

ACTIVITY 2

Your baby will be able to locate sounds and turn to see where they came from. Try to engage your baby by having conversations with her even when you're not sitting together or standing right in front of her.

DEVELOPMENTAL FOCUS

RECOMMENDED RESOURCES

Language Development

Conversation topic

_____

_____

_____

10 MINUTES   MONTH 5

ACTIVITY 3

Dad, it's time for another special daddy-baby bonding routine idea for the month. Try creating a character or a special voice that you speak in when doing tummy time with baby. You could be Tommy the Tummy Time Tiger who crawls around and softly roars while baby is wiggling around. Maybe you do a great parrot imitation: get a stuffed parrot and talk to baby with the parrot voice. Be creative. Have fun! This is your time to shine!

DEVELOPMENTAL FOCUS

RECOMMENDED RESOURCES

Daddy-Baby Bonding

Daddy and baby

_____
_____
_____

MAJORITY OF
WAKING MINUTES   MONTH 5

ACTIVITY 4

At this age your baby will gravitate towards and be interested in the colors and action on TV. However TV is not yet an appropriate teaching tool at this age. Colorful, playful, moving images will delight your child as entertainment. However, your baby still needs to have human interaction. Interpersonal socializing should be the core of her stimulation.

DEVELOPMENTAL
FOCUS

Language Development

RECOMMENDED
RESOURCES

Humans

9 MINUTES   MONTH 5

ACTIVITY 5

Engage your child with his environment by pointing out all the colors, objects, and actions around you. Talk about the colorful flowers. Describe the images on an advertisement. Share your random historical knowledge of the buildings or homes in your neighborhood. This will continue to be the easiest way to expose your baby to a lot of language and disparate vocabulary.

DEVELOPMENTAL FOCUS

Language Development

RECOMMENDED RESOURCES

Descriptive language

4 MINUTES   MONTH ⑤

ACTIVITY 6

What's the best thing you did as a parent so far this week? Write it down on a piece of paper in big fancy letters. Then hang it on the fridge for the whole family to see! Then take a picture and share it with your friends on social media. Celebrate YOU!

DEVELOPMENTAL FOCUS	RECOMMENDED RESOURCES
Fun!	Your best penmanship

_____

_____

_____

◔ 1 MINUTE   MONTH ⑤

ACTIVITY 7

If your baby is sitting up more then your doctor may recommend starting solid foods. You will want to consult your pediatrician. Keep in mind: at this age, solid foods are considered food that is pureed.

DEVELOPMENTAL
FOCUS

Nutrition

RECOMMENDED
RESOURCES

Doctor consultation

_____

_____

_____

⏱ 10 MINUTES   MONTH ⑤

ACTIVITY 8

Since birth your baby has been drinking milk in a reclined position. Now that baby is trying solid foods she should be sitting upright. In addition to talking to your doctor, ask other moms what they do and what their doctors recommend.

DEVELOPMENTAL FOCUS	RECOMMENDED RESOURCES
Nutrition	Crowdsourced information

_____

_____

_____

⏱ 1 MINUTE   MONTH ⑤

ACTIVITY 9

Your baby is starting to get stronger and you may notice him holding his own bottle. It requires strength, coordination and independence. This is a great skill to encourage.

DEVELOPMENTAL FOCUS	RECOMMENDED RESOURCES
Gross and Fine Motor Skills	**Bottle**

_____

_____

_____

1 MINUTE

MONTH (5)

ACTIVITY 10

If your baby isn't able to hold the bottle on his own it is not good to prop a bottle in his mouth. This can cause choking. Be patient; he will develop this skill in time.

DEVELOPMENTAL FOCUS

RECOMMENDED RESOURCES

Gross and Fine Motor Skills

Diligence

_____

_____

_____

⏱ 5 MINUTES   MONTH ⑤

ACTIVITY 11

Just a quick reminder: YOU are an incredible parent! We know how much you love your child and want the best for her. We're proud of you and so are all your friends and family!

DEVELOPMENTAL FOCUS

RECOMMENDED RESOURCES

Pride and Accomplishment

Time to reflect

_____

_____

_____

⏱ 2 MINUTES   MONTH ⑤

ACTIVITY 12

If your baby has teeth, this is a good time to start brushing her teeth with a dry brush to remove residue on her teeth. Be aware, though; she is still too young for toothpaste.

DEVELOPMENTAL FOCUS

Health and Hygiene

RECOMMENDED RESOURCES

Dentist approved infant toothbrush

5 MINUTES   MONTH 5

ACTIVITY 13

As more teeth are coming in your baby may be drooling more and wanting to chew on everything. Be sure to have chewing toys available. Also, be aware that putting things in his mouth is one of the ways that your baby is using all of his senses to investigate the world around him.

DEVELOPMENTAL
FOCUS

RECOMMENDED
RESOURCES

Physical Growth and
  Development

Teething toys

_____

_____

_____

20 MINUTES   MONTH 5

ACTIVITY 14

Time to check again to see if your home is still baby proofed. Crawl around on your hands and knees. Roll over on your back. See the world from your baby's point of view to check your cords, plugs, outlet, locking cabinets, security gates for steps, sharp corners, etc.

DEVELOPMENTAL
FOCUS

Baby Safety

RECOMMENDED
RESOURCES

Keen eyes

12 MINUTES   MONTH 5

ACTIVITY 15

Your baby will start becoming more mobile by rolling and scooting. She may start crawling, but it may not look like a traditional hands-and-knees crawl. That is okay! She has to develop all the muscles, balance, and coordination. That takes time. She will get it soon enough. Just keep encouraging her, and resist the urge to hand her everything just because she lets out a lil cry.

DEVELOPMENTAL
FOCUS

Gross Motor Skills

RECOMMENDED
RESOURCES

Encouragement

_____
_____
_____

5 MINUTES   MONTH **5**

Did you know that crawling is very important for trunk and upper body strength? It also develops a variety of motor development areas of the brain. Crawling also develops binocular vision. Looking far off then back to the immediate space is an important visual skill to learn.

DEVELOPMENTAL FOCUS

RECOMMENDED RESOURCES

Gross Motor Skills   **Safe area to crawl**

1 MINUTE   MONTH 5

ACTIVITY 17

Object permanence is when baby learns that mommy or daddy will leave and will return, or that a toy still exists even if you hide it behind a pillow or blanket. This skill begins right around this age.

DEVELOPMENTAL   RECOMMENDED
FOCUS   RESOURCES

Object Permanence   **Toy**

_____

_____

_____

ACTIVITY 18

One way to encourage development of object permanence is to play peek-a-boo. Pull a blanket over your head and then down again. Help baby to pull the blanket over her face and then down again. "Peek-a-boo!" Tickles and giggles will add to the fun.

DEVELOPMENTAL FOCUS

RECOMMENDED RESOURCES

Object Permanence

Blanket

3 MINUTES   MONTH 5

ACTIVITY 19

Babies may be a little vain. They really enjoy looking in the mirror to see their self. Looking in the mirror and touching the mirror is a fun game and begins the process of self-awareness. Really, though, they think they are seeing another baby.

DEVELOPMENTAL
FOCUS

Self-awareness

RECOMMENDED
RESOURCES

Mirror

_____

_____

_____

15 MINUTES   MONTH 5

ACTIVITY 20

Keep up the good work mom and dad! It is hard work to get everything done each day. And that's okay. Those bottles and dirty onesies will be there tomorrow (and the next day, and the next...). Give yourself a break. And while giving yourself a break, talk to your baby and show her a small sign of your love. Time out for a squeeze or an "I love you" is always worth it!

DEVELOPMENTAL FOCUS	RECOMMENDED RESOURCES
Love and Trust	Time out

15 MINUTES   MONTH 5

ACTIVITY 21

Play a game of "Baby Price is Right." Sitting on the floor, line up a group of 3 toys and let your baby see them. Then hide them behind 3 pillows. Whichever pillow he gestures towards first, bring out that toy for him to see and play with.

DEVELOPMENTAL FOCUS

RECOMMENDED RESOURCES

Fun!

Pillows and Toys

_____

_____

_____

Chris Drew, Ph.D.

PARENT'S NOTES
Advice from Our Readers
MONTH FIVE

LEAVING THE HOUSE

Michael D., Dad to Grayson, Los Angeles, CA

Remember the days when leaving the house to run an errand was a matter of putting on pants, tossing your keys, wallet, and phone in the pockets, and walking out the door?

Every now and then, when the wife and baby are asleep, I'll do just that: lace up some shoes, grab my keys and wallet, and head to CVS or walk to the Yumi Yogurt shop down the block by myself. I usually don't even want frozen yogurt or need anything from the store. I just want to remember what it's like to get up and go. No diaper bag. No formula. No baby wipes. No sippy cup. No musical toy that is singing the same mind-melting song for the 800th time. Just me, my shoes, my pants, my keys, and my wallet.

~ Michael D., Los Angeles, CA

PARENT WIN

Essential Activities
To Nurture Smarter Kids

THE FIRST YEAR

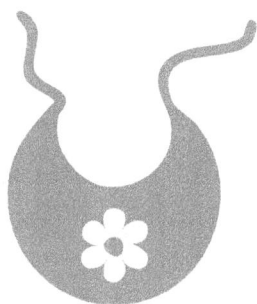

MONTH

10 MINUTES   MONTH 6

ACTIVITY 1

Car seat safety is important. It never hurts to double-check every now and then to be sure the seat is installed securely. And remember to keep your baby backward-facing in his car seat. Some states require facing backwards up to 18 months of age.

DEVELOPMENTAL FOCUS

RECOMMENDED RESOURCES

Baby Safety

Car seat manual

_____

_____

_____

Chris Drew, Ph.D.

10 MINUTES   MONTH 6

ACTIVITY 2

At this age your baby is not ready to speak words yet, but baby will start making sounds to simulate noises that sound like speech. Even though you may not understand what he is saying be sure to listen. Then respond when baby talks to you. He is learning conversational turn-taking.

DEVELOPMENTAL FOCUS

Conversational Turn-Taking

RECOMMENDED RESOURCES

Your voice and listening ears

5 MINUTES   MONTH 6

ACTIVITY 3

Baby's language skills will continue to flourish this month. Be sure to continue to introduce sign language: "more", "eat", and "all done" are all good signs to teach and review. "More" is signed by bringing together the fingers to your thumb on each hand and then tapping the tips together. "Eat" is signed by tapping your fingers and thumb on your mouth or chin. "All done" is signed by flicking your hands away from your body as if you are sweeping crumbs from the plate in front of you.

DEVELOPMENTAL FOCUS	RECOMMENDED RESOURCES
Language and Fine Motor Skills	Hand gestures

ACTIVITY 4

Baby is enjoying finger play at this age. Playing games like patty-cake and Itsy Bitsy Spider are great for developing hand-eye-coordination. If your baby is eating solids you can also try cutting food up into even tinier pieces to compel her to work on those pincher finger movements and coordination.

DEVELOPMENTAL FOCUS

Fine-motor skills

RECOMMENDED RESOURCES

Hands

15 MINUTES   MONTH 6

ACTIVITY 5

Dad, what is a memory you have of something you and your parents did with you? This month you can have your bonding-with-baby activity feature a special guest. Each Saturday or Tuesday night (or whenever) set a routine of calling one of your parents, a sibling, or a friend and have them re-enact a favorite story. If they can't be in person with you, you can have the other person on speaker phone, Skype, FaceTime, etc. Introduce the other person. Have the other person talk to baby. This will be a fun way to reconnect over old memories plus help baby socialize and build trust with your extended family.

DEVELOPMENTAL FOCUS

RECOMMENDED RESOURCES

Daddy-Baby Bonding   Daddy and baby

10 MINUTES   MONTH 6

ACTIVITY 6

We all have busy lives, and that's okay. It's normal. If you don't have time to do anything else during the day with your baby, simply talking and singing to him is great! Remember those early lessons in the book: quantity of words and diversity of language exposure will stimulate your baby's brain. This includes sharing new tones, pitches, volumes, and so on.

DEVELOPMENTAL
FOCUS

Language Development

RECOMMENDED
RESOURCES

Your voice

2 MINUTES   MONTH 6

ACTIVITY 7

Your baby starts to communicate in ways that anyone can understand: pointing and reaching to let you know what you want. Most likely the first thing she will learn to do is to reach her hands up indicating she wants to be held. Capture a photo of your baby expressing that she wants something by using her pointing or gesturing skills. Send it to your parents or siblings to show off your baby's developing communication skills.

DEVELOPMENTAL   RECOMMENDED
FOCUS   RESOURCES

**Language Develop-   Camera
ment**

🕐 10 MINUTES   MONTH 6

ACTIVITY 8

With the new skill of pointing it is a good idea to include books. Name the objects you're pointing at and help your baby point with you.

DEVELOPMENTAL FOCUS

RECOMMENDED RESOURCES

Language and Vocabulary Building

Book

---

20 MINUTES   MONTH 6

ACTIVITY 9

You will notice that your baby's Receptive Language (the ability to hear and understand what others are saying) develops prior to Expressive Language (the ability for baby to use words to fully express himself). This is obvious. What's important to keep in mind is that even though baby cannot speak the words she is hearing, she is still watching, absorbing, and learning a massive amount. So keep talking and using big words around baby.

DEVELOPMENTAL FOCUS	RECOMMENDED RESOURCES
Language Development	**Your vocabulary**

_____

_____

_____

5 MINUTES   MONTH 6

ACTIVITY 10

At this age baby may be starting to learn humor. Silly behavior such as peek-a-boo and other repetitive behaviors will bring a smile. What's a silly game your friends play with their babies or that your parents played with you?

DEVELOPMENTAL FOCUS

RECOMMENDED RESOURCES

Sense of humor

Sense of humor

_____

_____

_____

5 MINUTES   MONTH 6

ACTIVITY 11

Expressing humor demonstrates language learning. It is yet another way you can tell your child understands what is happening in his environment. What is something that really makes your baby laugh?

DEVELOPMENTAL
FOCUS

Language and Sense
of Humor

RECOMMENDED
RESOURCES

Sense of humor

_____

_____

_____

20 MINUTES　　　MONTH **6**

ACTIVITY 12

Try to read to your baby daily and continue to keep screen time at a minimum. Research shows that interaction with real, live humans is the superior way of stimulating your child and giving her every opportunity to learn from social interaction.

DEVELOPMENTAL FOCUS

Cognitive Development

RECOMMENDED RESOURCES

Social interaction

10 MINUTES   MONTH 6

ACTIVITY 13

Baby will still need to have tummy time. This is important for continued development of neck strength and upper body strength. What are some creative ways that you stimulate your baby while on her tummy? You can put books and toys in front of her. Try placing a stuffed animal or a toy that lights up or plays music. Of course, not every baby enjoys tummy time.

DEVELOPMENTAL FOCUS

Physical Strength

RECOMMENDED RESOURCES

Book or toy

_____

_____

_____

10 MINUTES   MONTH 6

ACTIVITY 14

Recall that infants use their mouth as a way of exploring their world. Baby will continue to mouth things to learn about objects. Be sure to have a variety of appropriate toys for baby to mouth or chew on. And watch out for coins or other small objects on the floor that baby could swallow.

DEVELOPMENTAL FOCUS

Cognitive Development

RECOMMENDED RESOURCES

Toys

5 MINUTES   MONTH 6

ACTIVITY 15

By now you baby will enjoy playing with objects more than ever. Baby will hold objects and may even pass the object from one hand to the other. If you model this behavior for your baby to imitate, he may try to copy you. Give it a try. And encourage him and celebrate when he does it with you!

DEVELOPMENTAL FOCUS

RECOMMENDED RESOURCES

Fine Motor Skills

Ball, toy, or other fun object

10 MINUTES   MONTH 6

ACTIVITY 16

Stack objects for your baby while describing the item by size, shape and color. Remember, you're building your baby's receptive language skills. Once items are stacked, baby will enjoy knocking over the stack of toys.

DEVELOPMENTAL FOCUS

RECOMMENDED RESOURCES

Language Skills and Fun

Stackable toys

_____

_____

_____

1,000s OF MINUTES   MONTH 6

ACTIVITY 17

By this age your baby has developed a strong attachment to his primary caregiver. He will feel comfortable with those who spend the most time with him. And baby will reach towards a favorite person when they appear.

DEVELOPMENTAL FOCUS	RECOMMENDED RESOURCES
Trust and Love	Love, affection, and time

_____

_____

_____

10 MINUTES   MONTH 6

ACTIVITY 18

As much as baby loves their primary caregiver she may have a fear of strangers, often crying when in the presence of unknown people. If baby is scared to go to a stranger, do not force baby to go. Instead talk to your baby and explain who the person is, and stay nearby your baby while the new person holds her. You can rub her back or hold her hand to help soothe her.

DEVELOPMENTAL
FOCUS

Trust and Socializing Skills

RECOMMENDED
RESOURCES

Patience

🕐 20 MINUTES　　　MONTH ⑥

ACTIVITY 19

Showing your baby that you like to read is one way to encourage literacy skills. By doing this you are modeling behavior and demonstrating positive habits that your baby will pick up on from an early age. Let your baby see you reading or working on your favorite hobby. The same is true for music, art, gardening, etc.

DEVELOPMENTAL FOCUS

RECOMMENDED RESOURCES

Pre-Literacy Skills

Books, newspapers, magazines, musical instrument, etc.

10 MINUTES   MONTH 6

ACTIVITY 20

Does your baby want to eat your book? At times she may only be interested in mouthing the book. That is okay. Make books and reading time a positive experience. Maybe you feel like snacking on the book as well. Be goofy. Have fun. The same is true with other new experiences, too: be positive!

DEVELOPMENTAL FOCUS	RECOMMENDED RESOURCES
Pre-Literacy Skills	Book

15 MINUTES   MONTH 6

ACTIVITY 21

What is your favorite inspirational quote, song, movie, etc.? Here is one example "Setting goals is the first step in turning the invisible into the visible." Write it on paper or hang up an image of it on your mirror for the week. Take a picture and share it with friends and family to encourage them, too. Share it with baby, too! Take her to the mirror and read it to her. Remember, baby is picking up the habits, attitudes, and values that you are demonstrating every day. Who knows, maybe baby had a tough morning with a busted rattle. Or maybe blankie somehow sleuthed away from her in the middle of the night. Maybe baby needs some motivation today, too!

DEVELOPMENTAL FOCUS

Motivation for Mom and Dad

RECOMMENDED RESOURCES

Inspirational quote

PARENT'S NOTES
Advice from Our Readers
MONTH SIX

OVERWHELMED

Trina F., Mom to Briana, Seattle, WA

I'm a badass working mother - or I would be... if:
- I had a personal assistant
- There were 48 hours in every day
- I owned a driverless car

My first two days back at work after 6 months maternity leave (generous I know), I felt like a rockstar. I could do this: have a successful career, a happy home life, and an active social life. That is before the *constant persistent* feeling of being *overwhelmed* set-in. I sit here writing this being back at work two weeks. TWO WEEKS! And let's be honest, I started feeling this way on Day 3.

I have learned that with only 24 hours in a day, I have time to shower: feed my baby, commute, work, pump at work (at least three times, no pressure!), pick-up from daycare, squeeze in 1-2 hours of quality baby time (best part of my day unless she sleeps through it in which case mom cries through it), cook dinner (after having to skip lunch because of a hectic work-day), pump (again!) work again, and if, and only if, I have the energy to unwind, swan dive into my bed, otherwise I just collapse (face unwashed, teeth unbrushed).

What I don't have time to do: sleep more than 4-6 hours a night (my baby sleeps 11, must be nice), read books on baby development, hang out with my new mom friends (because God knows I NEED them), make organic baby food, take self to doctor, do baby arts & crafts for family members to capture these moments (yeah right!), blow dry my hair, go to the grocery store, get waxed (sorry honey), manage family finances, make baby book (or at least find time to write down monthly height / weight), workout more than once a week.

I am expected to do all this AND not text and drive?!?! How on earth is everything supposed to get done!

~ Trina F., Seattle, WA

MONTH

10 MINUTES   MONTH ⑦

ACTIVITY 1

You may notice your baby whining or grunting more. This is because she is not able to communicate with words yet. But she is getting closer. Keep encouraging her by actively listening and talking back when baby talks to you.

DEVELOPMENTAL
FOCUS

RECOMMENDED
RESOURCES

Language Develop-
ment

Conversation

_____

_____

_____

5 MINUTES   MONTH 7

ACTIVITY 2

When your baby grunts or whines and points to an object, and you are able figure out what baby wants, say the word before giving the object to your baby. "Oh, you want your bottle? This is your bottle. Here you go. Be careful with your bottle." You may also want to emphasize the first syllable: "Buh, buh, bottle. Bottle starts with a B. Buh, buh, bottle."

DEVELOPMENTAL FOCUS

RECOMMENDED RESOURCES

Language and Phonics skills

Bottle or other favorite object

10 MINUTES   MONTH 7

ACTIVITY 3

Dad, what is your creative daddy-baby activity for this month? Each morning, before work, stand in front of the mirror and play daddy-a-boo (kind of like peek-a-boo). Stand in front of the mirror and talk and wave to baby and daddy (i.e. yourself). Smile, laugh, tickle, kiss. Then step to the side of the mirror: "Where's baby? Where's daddy?" Then step back in front of the mirror: "There they are!" You'll be teaching baby who daddy is as well as repeating the word and the person association. What are some iterations of this idea you could do?

DEVELOPMENTAL
FOCUS

RECOMMENDED
RESOURCES

Daddy–Baby Bonding   Daddy and baby

1,000s OF MINUTES   MONTH   7

ACTIVITY 4

Baby may be starting to or continuing to produce repetitive sounds at this age, things like "bababa". This is called babbling, and it is a precursor to forming speech. Your baby is still learning to master all the mouth and tongue muscles for speech. Imagine all the fine motor skills inside the mouth one has to master to form language – the tongue, teeth, lips, vocal cords, diaphragm, and more!

DEVELOPMENTAL FOCUS	RECOMMENDED RESOURCES
Language and Fine Motor Skills	Voice

3 MINUTES   MONTH 7

ACTIVITY 5

When your baby produces repetitive sounds hold up items that have that sound in it. You may also want to over-articulate the words as you say them. Be sure to let your baby see your mouth as you do so, so she can see and imitate how your forming the words with your mouth and tongue.

DEVELOPMENTAL
FOCUS

Phonics skills

RECOMMENDED
RESOURCES

Mouth and voice

_____

_____

_____

① 2 MINUTES   MONTH ⑦

ACTIVITY 6

Mom and Dad: Eat some pie.

DEVELOPMENTAL
FOCUS

Pleasure

RECOMMENDED
RESOURCES

Pie

🕐 3 MINUTES   MONTH ⑦

ACTIVITY 7

Songs with directions are helpful for transitions and for learning to follow directions. Songs offer a natural mnemonic device (a memorizing strategy). Plus the rhythms and rhymes make songs more fun. Can you think of direction songs like the "Hokey-Pokey"?

DEVELOPMENTAL FOCUS

Language Skills

RECOMMENDED RESOURCES

Songs

_____
_____
_____

🕐 3 MINUTES   MONTH 7

ACTIVITY 8

Make up a song for different activities that you do. You can have your own clean-up song to sing when you are finished playing. With fun lyrics and your own creative dance moves, everyone will knows what to do during clean-up!

DEVELOPMENTAL FOCUS	RECOMMENDED RESOURCES
Music, Family Bonding, and Fun	Creativity

_____

_____

_____

3 MINUTES   MONTH 7

ACTIVITY 9

Your baby may not know all the words, but they can still have fun dancing along to your songs. As you sing songs with directions, if the song says, "put your hands up," raise babies hands up!

DEVELOPMENTAL
FOCUS

Gross Motor Skills
and Dance Moves

RECOMMENDED
RESOURCES

Your jam

🕐 5 MINUTES   MONTH ⑦

ACTIVITY 10

We know that it's hard work raising kids. Your hard work and dedication shows up in the 100 little things you do each day. Even if others don't recognize it, we do! :-)

DEVELOPMENTAL FOCUS

Parent Recognition

RECOMMENDED RESOURCES

99 little things

_____

_____

_____

🕐 20 MINUTES   MONTH ⑦

ACTIVITY 11

Have you been exposing your child to lots of different music genres? Great! Now expose your child to lots of different types of art. Point out bright paintings, go touch different public sculptures, look at stained glass windows in churches. Art is everywhere. Of course your baby won't be internalizing the genius of Basquiat, DaVinci, or Picasso. But you will be modeling intellectual curiosity and cultural appreciation, the foundation of a love of learning.

DEVELOPMENTAL FOCUS

RECOMMENDED RESOURCES

Color Skills and Art Awareness

Art and awareness

_____

_____

_____

20 MINUTES   MONTH 7

ACTIVITY 12

Sometimes you don't necessarily need to read to your child, but let your child see you reading (or doing other positive activities). Your kids know what you value and will imitate those behaviors and come to value them as well.

DEVELOPMENTAL FOCUS	RECOMMENDED RESOURCES
Intellectual Curiosity	Your favorite intellectual endeavor

20 MINUTES   MONTH 7

ACTIVITY 13

Take a moment to reflect on one of your favorite family moments with your baby. Scroll through your pictures from the past few months and marvel at how you have matured as a parent and how your baby is growing. It's amazing, isn't it!

DEVELOPMENTAL
FOCUS

Celebration

RECOMMENDED
RESOURCES

Old photos

_____

_____

_____

🕐 10 MINUTES   MONTH ⑦

ACTIVITY 14

"You're off to Great Places! Today is your day! Your mountain is waiting, So...get on your way!" – Dr. Seuss. Mom and Dad, what mountain do you want to conquer in the next few days or weeks? Whatever goal you set, write it down; you can do it!

DEVELOPMENTAL FOCUS	RECOMMENDED RESOURCES
Goal setting	Pen and paper

_____

_____

_____

5 MINUTES   MONTH 7

ACTIVITY 15

What is the best piece of advice you could give, or the best piece of advice you have received from another parent? Share it with your friends and family. Send them a text message or an email.

DEVELOPMENTAL
FOCUS

Confidence

RECOMMENDED
RESOURCES

Advice

_____

_____

_____

5 MINUTES   MONTH 7

ACTIVITY 16

In addition to this book ;-), what is one of the best parenting resources, doctor recommendations, day care centers, or other tips you feel like other parents should know about? Post it on your social media or send it as a text to a friend.

DEVELOPMENTAL
FOCUS

Confidence

RECOMMENDED
RESOURCES

Advice

_____

_____

_____

① 1 MINUTE   MONTH ⑦

ACTIVITY 17

Research shows that if I smile and you see me and smile in response – even a very brief "micro-smile" – it's not just you imitating or empathizing with me. It may also be a way that I can pass on my happiness to you. This is called "motor mimicry."

DEVELOPMENTAL FOCUS	RECOMMENDED RESOURCES
Happiness	Smiles

_____

_____

_____

8 MINUTES   MONTH 7

ACTIVITY 18

Is baby restless or upset? Try passing on your happiness or calmness or other emotion on to your baby by smiling or taking deep breaths or just sitting and being calm. Try this with the adults in your life, too.

DEVELOPMENTAL
FOCUS

RECOMMENDED
RESOURCES

Calm and Emotional
Awareness

Deep breaths and
Zen-like state of mind

30 MINUTES   MONTH 7

ACTIVITY 19

Language is fundamentally a social act. The brain's language network properly and permanently wires up only when it is exposed to the coherent combination of sound, meaning, and grammar in any single human language – which is why it is so important to talk to your child as much as possible.

DEVELOPMENTAL FOCUS

Language Development

RECOMMENDED RESOURCES

Conversations and social setting

_____

_____

_____

Chris Drew, Ph.D.

30 MINUTES   MONTH 7

ACTIVITY 20

What are some social situations you can take your baby to so she can hear you with friends or other adults talking? Hold a Baby Congress where a group of parents get together, with babies in laps, and debate taxes, your favorite sports team or the latest fashion trend.

DEVELOPMENTAL FOCUS

RECOMMENDED RESOURCES

Language Development and Social Skills

Friends and a good topic of conversation

2 MINUTES   MONTH 7

ACTIVITY 21

Give your baby a string of compliments throughout the day: "You held the book all by yourself! You're so smart!" "You look so cute in that outfit." "You're so talkative today! Where did you learn all those words, you lil genius, you!?"

DEVELOPMENTAL FOCUS

RECOMMENDED RESOURCES

Confidence Building and Trust and Love

Kind, encouraging words

PARENT'S NOTES
Advice from Our Readers
MONTH SEVEN

CUDDLES AND KISSES
(Letter to Madison, July 30, 2017)

Chris D., Dad to Madison, San Mateo, CA

This past week you've been really under the weather. You've not been feeling well at all. You've had a fever and a cough. You haven't been sleeping well. And you refuse to be put down, which we don't mind, because each passing day you're becoming so much more independent with your walking. We love it when you're snuggly and wanting hugs. So sending you off to day care hasn't really been an option this week. Luckily Mommy and I were able to take turns staying with you.

Thursday night, about an hour after I put you to bed, you woke up very, very upset. You were so very sleepy, but you needed some more hugs. You just wanted to cuddle. Normally Mommy handles the consoling and the late night cuddling. But this rare occasion you wanted me for some reason.

So I picked you up out of bed and we just laid down on the floor next to your crib. We gathered up Bunny and

Mouse and Bear and Elephant and some other stuffed animal friends to use as pillows and leg rests. You nestled up into the crook of my arm and under my armpit. You laid there with Daddy and gently rolled back and forth or would kick your feet up onto my belly or would hold up bunny to give her a squeeze.
We laid on the floor for about an hour before you finally dozed off into a restful slumber.

Before you did, though, you rolled your head over to look at me. You pursed out your two perfect baby lips to give me the sweetest baby kisses I've ever had in my life. To this day this is the finest present and sweetest memory you have ever given me. Normally you save all your kisses for Mommy. You don't really give your Daddy many kisses. But when you do it lights up my entire week! And on this occasion you gave me FOUR of your perfect lil kisses.

I'm still on Cloud 9 just thinking about it and replaying our mini slumber party in my mind. I'm not sure if your fast-growing brain will hold moments and memories like these. But this tiny snapshot in time with you are the light of my life. Before your Mommy came along I never knew I could love so much. Before you came along I never knew how much joy I could have at one time. You may keep me from climbing mountains or going to comedy clubs or being able to leave the house in under 30 minutes every single time we go anywhere, but it is all worth it. You and your Mommy have lit up my life to shine on emotional parts of my heart that I didn't know existed.

So I guess what I'm trying to say is, thank you for our Thursday, 2:00 am slumber party.

~ Chris D., San Mateo, CA

PARENT WIN

Essential Activities
To Nurture Smarter Kids

THE FIRST YEAR

MONTH

2 MINUTES   MONTH 8

ACTIVITY 1

Baby has his own idea of what he wants to do and of what he may not want to do right away. Stay cool and do not raise your voice. Yelling will just get everyone upset.

DEVELOPMENTAL FOCUS

Patience

RECOMMENDED RESOURCES

Deep breaths

_____

_____

_____

⏱ 5 MINUTES   MONTH ⑧

ACTIVITY 2

Talk in a calm, soothing voice with your baby when they are upset. Loud talking or yelling continues to escalate the situation. Whisper pleasant words like "I love you." Maybe whistle Guns 'n' Roses "Patience." All together now, let's whistle it:…little paaatience. mm…yeah…need a little paa-atience. Mmm. …just a little pa-aaatience.

DEVELOPMENTAL FOCUS	RECOMMENDED RESOURCES
Patience	Whistling skills

10 MINUTES   MONTH 8

ACTIVITY 3

If you get frustrated as a parent and you feel that you may hurt your child, then place your child in his crib and take a break. It's okay. Everybody gets frustrated and everybody needs a break sometimes. I once read this story about Mother Teresa yelling at a fluffy Labradoodle puppy and chastising Pope John Paul II for his lavish footwear. ...it was a completely made up story. But it illustrated being human. None of us are perfect.

DEVELOPMENTAL   RECOMMENDED
FOCUS   RESOURCES

Patience   Crib and deep breaths

_____

_____

_____

8 MINUTES   MONTH 8

ACTIVITY 4

Baby will begin to enjoy cause-and-effect toys such as pushing buttons that light up. But baby may need help and demonstration from you. So show your baby how it is done and join in the play!

DEVELOPMENTAL FOCUS	RECOMMENDED RESOURCES
Cognitive Development	Cause and effect toys

_____

_____

_____

60 MINUTES   MONTH 8

ACTIVITY 5

Dad, what is your creative daddy-baby activity for this month? Phone a friend. Ask them what they do. Go have a beer or grab a coffee with a fellow new dad (or old dad). Moms are better at talking about their challenges, joys, frustrations, excitements about being a parent. A happy daddy is a great example for baby and is a huge support to mommy. It's also good to make a connection and socialize. Call up your new daddy buddy one time per week for the next 4 weeks. See what creative daddy-baby bonding ideas you can come up with.

DEVELOPMENTAL FOCUS	RECOMMENDED RESOURCES
Daddy-Baby Bonding	Daddy and baby

⏱ 2 MINUTES MONTH 8

ACTIVITY 6

As your baby begins to eat more, remember that breast milk and formula are still the primary source of nutrition.

DEVELOPMENTAL
FOCUS

RECOMMENDED
RESOURCES

Physical Development
and Nutrition

Baby formula and/or
breast milk

5 MINUTES   MONTH ⑧

ACTIVITY 7

Physical activity is important at every age. Moving baby's arms and legs is good exercise. Wave baby's arms in the air! (Like you just don't care!) Wiggle your waist. Kick those legs!

DEVELOPMENTAL FOCUS

RECOMMENDED RESOURCES

Physical Strength and Dexterity

Hands, arms, legs, feet

⏱ 5 MINUTES   MONTH 8

ACTIVITY 8

Have your baby stand with assistance. Hold her hands and dance! Go slow. Let baby shuffle her feet. Sing a song together. Now your turn: show baby your smooth moves while she watches. Dancing is a great way to exercise to build important muscles.

DEVELOPMENTAL
FOCUS

Physical Strength

RECOMMENDED
RESOURCES

Fun songs

3 MINUTES   MONTH 8

ACTIVITY 9

Play the game "Head, shoulders knees and toes." Move baby's hands to touch each body parts for exercise. Be sure to say each body part as you touch it.

DEVELOPMENTAL FOCUS

RECOMMENDED RESOURCES

Body Awareness and Gross Motor Skills

Body and gestures

_____

_____

_____

⏱ 10 MINUTES   MONTH 8

ACTIVITY 10

Play hide-and-seek. Move behind objects and have baby crawl to find you as you peek out. Tell baby to point: "Where's mommy?" "Show me where brother is!?" Way to go, baby! Giver her a hug. Now move to another spot and hide. (If you don't let baby see where you went, then use your voice so she can spot you.)

DEVELOPMENTAL FOCUS

RECOMMENDED RESOURCES

Physical Strength

Not-so-good hiding spots ;-)

_____

_____

_____

10 MINUTES   MONTH 8

ACTIVITY 11

While reading books make the sounds of the animals and the gadgets that you see. You can make reading an interactive activity by imitating the motions of the animals in the stories: walk like an elephant and swing your trunk; waddle like a duck and flick your tail; gallop like a horse and say, "neeiiigh."

DEVELOPMENTAL
FOCUS

RECOMMENDED
RESOURCES

Cognitive Development and Pre-Literacy Skills

Book and creativity

10 MINUTES   MONTH 8

ACTIVITY 12

While riding in the car tell baby when you are turning left or right or when you are going to slow down or speed up. Keep the conversation going wherever you are. You can even tell baby about your day.

DEVELOPMENTAL FOCUS

Language Development

RECOMMENDED RESOURCES

Your voice

MONTH 8

ACTIVITY 13

Tell baby what you are doing when you are getting baby out of the stroller or car seat. "Okay, get ready: I'm unsnapping and pulling your arms out. Grab your bottle!" Our baby went through a period when she hated her car seat and would bend and stiffen her body in impossibly contorted poses of protest. We tried everything. One thing that started working was when we would patiently explain that we're about to go for a ride and would love for her to join us by riding in her car seat. We would also ask her to help us by holding a toy or object. Weirdly, this combination bit of diplomacy eventually brought about peace in the land.

DEVELOPMENTAL FOCUS

Language Skills and Cooperation

RECOMMENDED RESOURCES

Mommy and Daddy Diplomacy

⏱ 2 MINUTES   MONTH ⑧

ACTIVITY 14

When you go out be sure you take some teachable items like books and simple cause and effect toys for baby to play with. You never know when you might get stuck in a line and need to be an entertainer!

DEVELOPMENTAL FOCUS	RECOMMENDED RESOURCES
Social skills	Toys

_____

_____

_____

5 MINUTES   MONTH 8

ACTIVITY 15

When going on short trips take with you items and toys baby is used to. He will feel more comfortable. For emergency situations, you can keep a new toy hidden in your trunk or diaper bag. Assuming he is not hungry or sick, pull it out for a moment when baby is having a total nuclear meltdown to see if the new toy can distract him.

DEVELOPMENTAL FOCUS	RECOMMENDED RESOURCES
Superparenting	**Secret toy stash**

75 MINUTES   MONTH 8

ACTIVITY 16

Be sure to take some time for yourself and your significant other. You are busy with all that you do for baby, but you have to set aside time to take care of yourself, too. Sneak away for a massage or to get your nails done. Go out and watch a game with the fellas.

DEVELOPMENTAL FOCUS	RECOMMENDED RESOURCES
Superparenting	Babysitter and/or understanding spouse

PARENT'S NOTES
Advice from Our Readers
MONTH EIGHT

STICKING TOGETHER

Wendy R., Mom to Sophia, New York, NY

Bet you saw that header and thought of your husband. It's true, I do think you have to try to put your marriage first. But what I'm talking about is Mom's. We are a special breed who others sometimes don't understand, including our husbands.

Having children is wonderful, awe-inspiring, joy-bringing, eye-opening (in the best way), heart-bursting, love-fests all day long. It's also hard. Really hard. And each person has a different struggle: colic, not sleeping, teething, medical issues, weight loss issues, won't take a bottle, sensitive kids, emotional kids, clingy kids...

Some days we are working our butts off just to keep this bundle of constant extremes alive. Next time you see that mom at the store, baby on one hip, toddler screaming and crying in a fit of nonsense, it's probably me. And sometimes, even though we are superhero moms in a multitude of ways, we need encouragement from those who understand most. So instead of walking by with some kind of look on your face, stop and tell that mom she's doing a great job, tell her you're taking notes, tell her she's your hero. Be uplifting. We need it!

~ Wendy R., New York, NY

PARENT WIN

*Essential Activities
To Nurture Smarter Kids*

THE FIRST YEAR

MONTH

1,000s OF MINUTES   MONTH 9

ACTIVITY 1

By age 9 months baby is forming object permanence, which demonstrates baby has short term memory or short term recall. He will look for things that were last seen even when he can't see them.

DEVELOPMENTAL FOCUS	RECOMMENDED RESOURCES
Object Permanence	None

_____

_____

_____

10 MINUTES   MONTH 9

ACTIVITY 2

Dad, what's your special dad-baby thing for this month? One idea to consider: Going for walks with baby on your shoulders. By now, baby is getting strong enough to balance himself when sitting up straight. Each time you go outside for a short morning or evening walk around the block, put junior on your shoulders. "You want up, up? Okay, 1, 2, 3, weeee." Baby will love being higher up and having the new perspective on top of daddy's head. Be sure to hold on tight and be prepared for any sudden lurches of excitement.

DEVELOPMENTAL FOCUS	RECOMMENDED RESOURCES
Daddy-Baby Bonding	Daddy and baby

3 MINUTES   MONTH 9

ACTIVITY 3

Object permanence demonstrates baby has short-term memory and recall. Put a toy on the table and then put a cereal box, pillow, purse or something else in front of it. Does baby try to look behind the box?

DEVELOPMENTAL FOCUS	RECOMMENDED RESOURCES
Object Permanence	Toy

_____

_____

_____

7 MINUTES   MONTH 9

ACTIVITY 4

Recall is important in pre-literacy and literacy skills. Baby will start to use this skill to recall information from books, which is essential for reading comprehension.

DEVELOPMENTAL FOCUS	RECOMMENDED RESOURCES
Cognitive Development and Pre-literacy Skills	Books

10 MINUTES   MONTH 9

ACTIVITY 5

Cut up an orange, a tomato, and cilantro. From your cabinet get your cinnamon, basil, and pepper. Line up six jars or small containers on the table and put the pieces into each jar. Now take turns smelling the contents. Describe the object and its scent to your child. Let them touch it, feel it, and taste. They probably won't know how to sniff things yet, so be sure to demonstrate for them and describe what you're doing. Then have them imitate you. If you don't have these fruits, veggies, or spices, use whatever else you may have around the kitchen.

DEVELOPMENTAL FOCUS

Sensory Development and Language Development

RECOMMENDED RESOURCES

Small containers with spices, flower petals, fruit pieces, etc.

🕐 5 MINUTES   MONTH 9

ACTIVITY 6

To work on object permanence, you don't need fancy or expensive games. While playing with baby, simply put a blanket over a toy and ask baby, "Where is it?"

DEVELOPMENTAL
FOCUS

RECOMMENDED
RESOURCES

Object Permanence   Toy and Blanket

60 MINUTES   MONTH 9

ACTIVITY 7

Establishing routines with baby are important for mom and dad's sanity (e.g. a regular bed time!). But routines are also important for baby because they help provide a sense of security and predictability – both of which are essential to development. You have already been establishing routines with baby over the past few months. What are some of the most effective, or best routines you have with your baby? What are some routines that you know other parents do?

DEVELOPMENTAL FOCUS	RECOMMENDED RESOURCES
Security and Predictability	Routines and habits

_____

_____

_____

2 MINUTES   MONTH 9

ACTIVITY 8

Before reading to your baby ask baby where the books are. Wait for baby to respond. Help baby point to where you keep your books. You can do this during dinner-time, when it's time to do a diaper change, or whenever. Think about how you involve baby for other routines, too, by having her identify other objects that are associated with specific events, for example towels with bath time, bibs for eating, car seat for making trips, etc. Have baby help you prepare for the routines and become a contributor.

DEVELOPMENTAL FOCUS

Language Development, Spatial Awareness

RECOMMENDED RESOURCES

Space for keeping books

2 MINUTES   MONTH ⑨

ACTIVITY 9

At this age baby is beginning to learn that his actions have an impact on his environment. Other than crying or grunting to get your attention, what are some ways your baby is consciously impacting things around him? Be sure to interact with him in a conversational manner that you want him to eventually adopt. If baby is reaching and grabbing to get out of his high chair, say to baby: "Are you done? Okay, raise your hands and say, 'Up, please.' That's good!"

DEVELOPMENTAL
FOCUS

Language Development, Social Skills

RECOMMENDED
RESOURCES

Conversational responses

_____

_____

_____

10 MINUTES   MONTH 9

ACTIVITY 10

It is important to be aware of the behaviors, attitudes, values, and habits you are reinforcing with your child. If baby screams, do you run to get milk? Or do you wait for him to use his sign language? Does baby see you speaking calmly or raising your voice at others? Does baby see you say please and thank you to your spouse? Does baby see you being kind when stuck in traffic? When baby is with you does he see you constantly distracted by your phone or the television? The things baby sees and hears are the behaviors, attitudes, values, and habits he will adopt.

DEVELOPMENTAL FOCUS

RECOMMENDED RESOURCES

Personality Development

Awareness of your actions

(⏱) 2 MINUTES   MONTH (9)

ACTIVITY 11

Reinforce appropriate communication efforts. If your baby tries to sign for milk, respond to her, "Yes, milk. Good job!" And to reinforce the sign language, you should make the sign, too.

DEVELOPMENTAL FOCUS

RECOMMENDED RESOURCES

Language Development

Awareness

_____

_____

_____

10 MINUTES   MONTH 9

ACTIVITY 12

Create a play time by getting out pots, pans, spoons, ladles, etc. and have baby bang on a pot or pan. Cover your ears and say, "That's really loud." Or "That is a lovely tune you are playing!" Take a tour of the kitchen and show baby the stove and say, "That's hot. Ouch! We don't touch hot stoves." Show baby the freezer and say, "That's really cold. Brrrr!" Continue this routine other sensory experiences around the house: soft pillows, rough door mats, wet bathtubs, dark closets, noisy laundry rooms, etc.

DEVELOPMENTAL FOCUS	RECOMMENDED RESOURCES
Sensory development	Household objects

10 MINUTES   MONTH 9

ACTIVITY 13

Play tug o' war to build strength and balance. When baby is holding a blanket give it a soft tug. When baby tugs back over-exaggerate like you're being pulled in baby's direction :-)

DEVELOPMENTAL   RECOMMENDED
FOCUS   RESOURCES

Gross Motor Skills   Towel or pillow cover

5 MINUTES   MONTH 9

ACTIVITY 14

At this age baby will begin to be more flexible in imitation skills. In other words, baby will not have to see herself doing an action in order to imitate what they see someone else doing. Stick out your tongue and wiggle it around. Have baby try it. Pat your mouth as you say "Ahhh-hhhhhh". Help baby pat his mouth as he says "ahhhhhhhh". Practice blowing kisses or waving goodbye, etc. Baby will start to imitate these actions himself.

DEVELOPMENTAL FOCUS	RECOMMENDED RESOURCES
Gross Motor Skills	Your body

10 MINUTES   MONTH 9

ACTIVITY 15

Test your baby's flexibility with imitation skills. While playing, make faces at baby. See if she makes faces back at you. Take a picture of a funny face your baby makes. You can also head to the bathroom and play this game in the mirror.

DEVELOPMENTAL
FOCUS

RECOMMENDED
RESOURCES

Gross Motor Skills   **You and baby**

_____

_____

_____

60 MINUTES   MONTH 9

ACTIVITY 16

Is there a state park, a museum, or something historic about where you live? There is likely free (or really cheap) admission to go on a mini family field trip to one of these places. It will give the grown ups (and older kids) a chance to be stimulated while also taking baby on a new adventure. Explain to baby how you are interacting with the museum or park, how you talk to the rangers or docents. Baby will love the new experience!

DEVELOPMENTAL FOCUS	RECOMMENDED RESOURCES
Social Skills, Language Skills	Park or museum

8 MINUTES   MONTH 9

ACTIVITY 17

At this age baby is taking interest in more details of objects. Baby will engage in items for longer periods of time as she is able to keep her attention on a specific activity or toy. Encourage this focus by staying focused with baby on her favorite toy or by having a conversation as you are doing an activity together.

DEVELOPMENTAL FOCUS	RECOMMENDED RESOURCES
Cognitive development	Favorite toy

_____

_____

_____

Chris Drew, Ph.D.

30 MINUTES   MONTH 9

ACTIVITY 18

By now baby is interested in objects for longer periods of time, but this does not mean that baby will start playing by himself just yet. In fact, most of baby's time will be spent jumping from one exploration to the next. As baby starts to become more mobile she still needs a play partner and the close, watchful eye of an adult. By baby-proofing a room or a space in your house you can allow baby to be inquisitive while also getting a few of your own chores done.

DEVELOPMENTAL FOCUS

Cognitive development

RECOMMENDED RESOURCES

Baby proofing

249

5 MINUTES   MONTH 9

ACTIVITY 19

Take advantage of baby's new interest. What is something that your baby seems to be paying a lot of attention to? When out to dinner present baby with this new object or an object he hasn't seen a few days. This could provide some quiet time as baby focuses on her favorite thing.

DEVELOPMENTAL FOCUS

Reprieve for Mommy and Daddy

RECOMMENDED RESOURCES

Favorite toy

2 MINUTES   MONTH 9

ACTIVITY 20

To keep baby's interest in objects be sure to rotate a variety of toys for her to play with. Keep some toys put away for a few days and then bring them out again. To her they will seem like new toys.

DEVELOPMENTAL FOCUS	RECOMMENDED RESOURCES
Tip for Mommy and Daddy	Good hiding spot

_____

_____

_____

20 MINUTES   MONTH 9

ACTIVITY 21

You do not need to buy lots and lots of toys. The same is true with books. Take advantage of your library. Or do a book swap with friends. Just as you do with baby's toys, rotate the books you read. Baby will be excited to see "new" books every few days.

DEVELOPMENTAL
FOCUS

RECOMMENDED
RESOURCES

Cognitive Development

Books, toys, library, friends

20 MINUTES   MONTH 9

ACTIVITY 22

Taking baby out to dinner with you can teach valuable social and etiquette skills. You can also do this at home. Invite friends over to do a formal meal or tea time play date. Baby is still really young, but you're exposing him to positive, healthy behaviors. Remember, baby picks up on your behaviors, mannerisms, and ways of being.

DEVELOPMENTAL FOCUS	RECOMMENDED RESOURCES
Social Skills	Friends, family, acquaintances

_____

_____

_____

PARENT'S NOTES
Advice from Our Readers
MONTH NINE

HOW DO I FREEZE TIME?

Grace B., Mom to Athena, Santa Barbara, CA

We've all heard it, right? - from the time we were first pregnant to as recent as this morning when I was proudly showing pictures of my daughter to the gal in line with me at Starbucks. "Enjoy it. It's short and goes way too fast!"

I used to hear these "words of wisdom" and chalk them up to unwanted advice - in one ear and out the other. Like the time my mother told me that my breastmilk might be causing my daughter's colic. These words particularly did not resonate with me when I was pregnant with my head in every toilet in town for 5 months. Those days couldn't go fast enough.

But now, as I stare at my daughter at 9 months and realize how much she's changed from those 8 month pictures on my wall, I realize how truly fast this time is flying by. She learns something new daily and we seem to get to know each other better as time goes on. I am now officially one of those parents who wants to stop time.

But how? I've spent many a sleepless night with this question. I try to cherish every moment with her - every smile that warms my heart, the feeling I get sharing in her joy when she does something for the first time. Simultaneously, trying to figure out how to deal with her mini-tantrums that sweep over her as if she were an irrational toddler - losing her baby mind when she's suddenly decides no, she does not want to get in her car seat for what must seem like the millionth time in her short life - makes me want to run for the hills. Thinking about her being a toddler makes me want to run even farther!

I've noticed that time goes slower when it's just the two of us together hanging out. It goes slower when I'm not trying to multi-task around the house, on my phone, mentally somewhere else. Time seems to go slower when we do something she wants to do (walk 1 mile to the park so she can swing and watch the big kids for all of 10 minutes). It goes slower when I sneak into her room at night to watch her sleeping peacefully - the thought of which brings me to tears as I write it.

Being present with all we have to do as moms seems an impossible task - our minds one incessant, never-ending "To-Do" list. But darnit, I'm a MOM and I'm going to try - even if it's just for a few minutes every day. I won't remember what she looked like at 10 months or when she met certain "milestones" and I certainly won't remember that email I was reading when we were playing in her room. But I'll remember this feeling - the joy I feel when looking at my daughter, the light of my life, when I am truly present in her journey.

~ Grace B., Santa Barbara, CA

MONTH

5 MINUTES   MONTH 10

ACTIVITY 1

It's always a good idea to do a safety check for things that could hurt baby. For example, check the fit of your child's car seat. Is it still snuggly and properly installed in your car? If you've had to remove and then reinstall the seat, or even as the weather changes, you should double check belts and straps to loosen or tighten them as needed.

DEVELOPMENTAL FOCUS	RECOMMENDED RESOURCES
Car Safety	Safety instructions

2 MINUTES   MONTH 10

ACTIVITY 2

What are some of your safe driving habits? Do you pull over and stop before reaching back to try to hand baby the bottle she dropped? Do you put your cell phone away? What's another safe driving habit you have? Buying a rear-facing mirror to attach to the back seat is a great way to let baby keep her eye on you (and vice versa). This simple little purchase can provide peace of mind, entertainment, and just generally let you know what's going on back there with baby!

DEVELOPMENTAL FOCUS

Mommy and Daddy peace of mind

RECOMMENDED RESOURCES

Backseat baby mirror

10 MINUTES   MONTH 10

ACTIVITY 3

Most insurance companies offer safe driving tips on their websites or in the agents' offices. Call your insurance agent to tell them you want to be the safest driver out there! And tell them to make a note to your account. And while you have them on the phone, try to see if they'll give a new parent a break on your rates. ;-)

DEVELOPMENTAL
FOCUS

RECOMMENDED
RESOURCES

Family Safety

Insurance provider

Chris Drew, Ph.D.

30 MINUTES   MONTH 10

ACTIVITY 4

Does your baby fall asleep easily in the car? If so, on those sleepless nights when she simply won't fall asleep in her crib, consider taking her for an evening ride. It can be a good excuse for Mom and Dad to grab a chocolate milkshake or some other treat you deserve.

DEVELOPMENTAL FOCUS

Mommy and Daddy peace of mind

RECOMMENDED RESOURCES

Car

261

ACTIVITY 5

While in the kitchen making dinner, you can let baby play alongside you. Get out a pot or pan. Grab a spoon, ladle, or stirrer. Show baby how when you bang on the pot with the wooden spoon it makes a different noise than when you bang with a metal ladle. Let baby explore the sounds while you do your thing!

DEVELOPMENTAL FOCUS

RECOMMENDED RESOURCES

Gross motor skills

Pot, pan, ladle, spoon

_____

_____

_____

20 MINUTES   MONTH 10

ACTIVITY 6

What are some of your most effective travel tricks that keep your baby calm and occupied while you're in the car? For us, singing and making sure Madison has something to occupy her hands are two key strategies. We try to reserve one of her favorite toys to play with during car rides, and for longer rides we try to time them with one of her sleep times.

DEVELOPMENTAL FOCUS	RECOMMENDED RESOURCES
Sanity for Mommy and Daddy	Favorite toy or sleep time timing

_____

_____

_____

2 MINUTES   MONTH 10

ACTIVITY 7

If he hasn't already, soon your baby will start to form attachments to favorite toys, books, blankets, etc. Be careful about what you allow him to sleep with, especially if you think there is a suffocation hazard associated with it.

DEVELOPMENTAL FOCUS	RECOMMENDED RESOURCES
Safety	Choking hazard awareness

_____

_____

_____

ACTIVITY 8

The more reinforcement you give when baby attempts to communicate with gestures and sounds, the more likely she will try again to communicate using those same gestures or sounds. If she wants water or a banana or whatever it may be, repeat the name of the thing and point to it. Be sure to respond quickly and positively to the communication attempts you want to hear from her.

DEVELOPMENTAL FOCUS	RECOMMENDED RESOURCES
Language Development	Gestures and naming

2 MINUTES   MONTH 10

ACTIVITY 9

News flash: You have one of the most important jobs in the world, and you're doing a fantastic job at it! Way to go mom and dad! We appreciate all you do. And so does your baby!

DEVELOPMENTAL FOCUS	RECOMMENDED RESOURCES
Kudos for Mom and Dad	Pat on the back

_____

_____

_____

10 MINUTES   MONTH 10

ACTIVITY 10

Baby will want to include you in his discovery of new objects. And research has shown baby will attend to objects longer when a caregiver is looking and participating too. Share in his discovery by acknowledging and encouraging, and pay attention to objects or activities that your baby enjoys.

DEVELOPMENTAL FOCUS

RECOMMENDED RESOURCES

Social Skills, Bonding

Caregiver attention

2 MINUTES   MONTH 10

ACTIVITY 11

Are you finding this book to be a super helpful resource? If so, tell a friend or family member. Share the love! :-)

DEVELOPMENTAL
FOCUS

Parental bonding

RECOMMENDED
RESOURCES

Word of mouth

_____
_____
_____

⏱ 2 MINUTES   MONTH ⑩

ACTIVITY 12

Baby will want to include mom and dad in his activities. And there are several ways he will do so. The first is by holding/showing an object to you for you to look at, but not to take. He's proud and wants to share with you. One example of this is during meal times your baby may try to put his food in your mouth. He's imitating all the times you have fed him!

DEVELOPMENTAL FOCUS	RECOMMENDED RESOURCES
Social Skills	Food or other favorite objects

_____

_____

_____

10 MINUTES   MONTH 10

ACTIVITY 13

An evolution of holding/showing objects is for baby to include mom and dad in activities by holding out an object. She will give you her toy or some other object, but she may want it back quickly. Sharing isn't quite a concept that baby has yet. However, be sure to tell her thank you when she gives it to you!

DEVELOPMENTAL FOCUS	RECOMMENDED RESOURCES
Social Skills	**Toy**

_____

_____

_____

Chris Drew, Ph.D.

⏱ 2 MINUTES   MONTH ⑩

ACTIVITY 14

Another way your baby will want to include mom and dad in activities is by reaching or leaning towards you or an object. This is a form of requesting. While baby is engaging in these behaviors it is appropriate for you to follow the communicative lead of the child. Reinforce baby's "ask" by responding with conversation, again, naming the thing/activity baby is reaching for, talking about it, and handing it to him. Remember, say Please and Thank You. :-)

DEVELOPMENTAL FOCUS

Language Development

RECOMMENDED RESOURCES

Language

10 MINUTES   MONTH 10

ACTIVITY 15

Another way your baby will want to include mom and dad in activities is by pointing. Baby wants to show you something or go somewhere. Whichever it is, show your interest in exploring that thing with him. Name the thing, place, or activity and point at it (or do the activity). As well, the things that are baby's favorite are those things that he sees around him most (or sees you doing). You can get baby's interest in something by doing that thing yourself in front of baby and smiling and laughing and showing how much fun you are having by doing it. For example, if you want baby to start liking books or drinking water, start holding/reading books around baby even when not playing with him. Start carrying a water bottle around and drinking more water. ...you get the idea.

DEVELOPMENTAL FOCUS	RECOMMENDED RESOURCES
Language Development, Social Skills	**Objects or activities**

10 MINUTES   MONTH 10

ACTIVITY 16

By now you're picking up on baby's communications and hopefully baby is relying less on crying as her way to communicate all her needs. You guys are doing a great job of developing communication channels. Way to go!

DEVELOPMENTAL
FOCUS

Language Development

RECOMMENDED
RESOURCES

Pats on the back

_____

_____

_____

15 MINUTES   MONTH 10

ACTIVITY 17

Using gestures and facial expressions to tell a story with or without the book can be an interesting and fun way to engage your child so that your child has to learn to look at you for clues to a story.

Can you retell the story of Goldilocks and the three bears? Tell this story without the book. Try to integrate as much body language and gestures as possible. Get creative being a bear, eating cold porridge, tacking a nap in a hard bed, etc. Give it a try.

DEVELOPMENTAL FOCUS

RECOMMENDED RESOURCES

Language Development

Gestures and creativity

30 MINUTES   MONTH 10

ACTIVITY 18

After retelling a familiar story a few times with repetitive gestures, stop to see if baby can fill in the missing gesture, sound, or facial expression. This is a great way to exhibit listening comprehension skills.

DEVELOPMENTAL
FOCUS

RECOMMENDED
RESOURCES

**Language Develop-
ment**

Gestures

🕐 5 MINUTES   MONTH ⑩

ACTIVITY 19

Sing the itsy bitsy spider song with hand gestures. After several repetitions, help baby do some of the gestures. Finger dexterity is an important fine motor skill to work on.

DEVELOPMENTAL
FOCUS

RECOMMENDED
RESOURCES

Fine Motor Skills   Song and gestures

ACTIVITY 20

Get a candle and matches. Strike the match and then blow it out. Talk about what is happening as the match head rubs across the friction of the match box: heat is created and a flame starts burning. Now blow it out and describe the smoke and the smell. Light the match again and describe the flame. Now light the candle and have baby help you blow out the match. If baby hasn't seen a striking match or burning candle before she will be mesmerized by the process and by the flame. Be sure to describe the fire as Hot. (This is how Madison learned the word "hot".) Don't touch! It will cause an ouchie. And, of course, be careful and make sure to blow out the candle and keep it out of reach of baby.

Chris Drew, Ph.D.

DEVELOPMENTAL FOCUS	RECOMMENDED RESOURCES
Language Development	**Match and candle**

10 MINUTES   MONTH 10

ACTIVITY 21

Another effective way to continue to work on baby's fine motor skills is to cut up her food into smaller pieces. Baby should be using her pinchers to grab things between her pointer finger and thumb. During meal time she can work on being precise with her grabbing and picking. Over time you'll see the refinement of this skill start to manifest elsewhere, for example in how she is able to turn the pages of a book one page at a time.

DEVELOPMENTAL   RECOMMENDED
FOCUS   RESOURCES

Fine Motor Skills   Food

20 MINUTES   MONTH 10

ACTIVITY 22

Do you have a shape sorter, a way for your child to place different size shapes into different openings? Play with shape sorters by having your child put different sized balls (or other shapes) in the different size openings. You can do this with cookie cutters from the kitchen, small blocks of scrap wood, sticks from the yard, even Jell-O shapes (if you have a ton of spare time on your hand ;-). This is another great way to work on fine motor skills and descriptive language.

DEVELOPMENTAL FOCUS	RECOMMENDED RESOURCES
Fine Motor Skills	Different shaped objects

10 MINUTES   MONTH 10

ACTIVITY 23

Putting different shapes into a container with cut outs can be a big challenge for baby. With this game, watch to notice whether your child gives up, gets frustrated, keeps trying or looks for your help. Work alongside your baby to solve the problem. Show baby how you match the shape to the cut out in the container. It's okay if baby doesn't get it, or if she just wants to chuck the shapes across the room. That can be just as fun. Plus, let's be honest, there are days you want to just chuck the shapes across the room, too ;-)

DEVELOPMENTAL FOCUS	RECOMMENDED RESOURCES
Fine Motor Skills	Block shapes

PARENT'S NOTES
Advice from Our Readers
MONTH TEN

OVERWHELMED: WHO AM I AT 2 AM?

Laura B., Mom to Lilly, Redwood City, CA

My daughter is almost 11 months old, and she still wakes up twice a night to eat. Sometimes she wakes up 1 or 2 additional times just to let us know she is still here for a few minutes of squawking before putting herself back to sleep.

Yes, babies who do not sleep through the night for a long time exist and, therefore, parents who do not sleep through the night for a seemingly infinite amount of time exist, too. And getting to know myself as a parent who is awake multiple times a night in the wee hours of the morning on a daily basis was a scary thing.

I had braced myself for the post-partum sleep deprivation marathon for which there is no clear "finish line," but I had not steeled myself to the Dr. Jekel/Mr. Hyde transformation that occurred inside me in the dark of night. By day, I considered myself to be an optimistic, patient, level-headed person and a sweet, loving wife.

However, between the hours of 11 PM and 4 AM, all that went out the window. This was the perfect time to be really passive aggressive to my husband (Yes, that stealing of the blanket was intentional and, Yes, I meant to stomp back into the room after nursing our child) as well as the ideal opportunity to actively pick a fight (of course, it had to be about something that either happened at least a year ago or that I pretty much made up in my head).

These wee hours also proved to be the time most conducive for questioning all my life-decisions ranging anywhere from what I ate for dinner that night to what I chose for a career 10 years prior. Invariably, during this time, I would field a litany of self-criticisms and self-doubt as I thought about all the other sleeping babies who had been successfully sleep trained by their parents who were clearly more qualified than I to be raising a child.

Eventually, I would accumulate about 6 hours of broken sleep and wake up, feeling mostly back to my normal self, but always more than just a bit confused over and practically hungover by what had happened to me between 11 PM and 4 AM.

~ Laura B., Redwood City, CA

MONTH

5 MINUTES   MONTH 11

ACTIVITY 1

At this age your child will love animal books. While looking at the animals on each page, do the animal noises. Even though she will love it, sometimes it gets a little old for Mom and Dad. To spice things up, do Upside Down animal noises! For example, turn the book upside down and read it from a different perspective. The cow say, "oooom" instead of "mooo". The hen says, "doodle oodle cock" instead of "cockle doodle do". Make it more fun for yourself while demonstrating creativity to your child.

DEVELOPMENTAL FOCUS	RECOMMENDED RESOURCES
Creative thinking	Animal book

3 MINUTES   MONTH **11**

ACTIVITY 2

Increasingly baby is coming to grasp cause and effect. Each day she is trying (and succeeding) to figure out things on her own. Help her accelerate that! Buckles, buttons, snaps, lights, radios, etc. require fine motor skills (cause) to manipulate them to have an effect. Show baby how to twist a nob to turn on the radio. Show her how to press the release button on a seat belt. Demonstrate how flipping a light switch turns the lights on/off. Describe what is happening when you perform an action and what happens as a result.

DEVELOPMENTAL FOCUS	RECOMMENDED RESOURCES
Cognitive Development	Buckles, buttons, snaps, lights, radios, etc

45 MINUTES   MONTH 11

ACTIVITY 3

Not all babies are walking at this age. However, your baby may be starting to stand or attempting to "cruise" (hold on to furniture as she takes steps). Now is time to think about phase two of baby-proofing the house. Don't leave scissors on your coffee table. Move breakable objects beyond baby's outstretched (standing!) reach. Steps or minor declines are also a hazard. In addition to simply not being able to pay attention, baby's understanding of sudden inclines/declines is still developing. So safeguard against tripping hazards, too.

DEVELOPMENTAL FOCUS	RECOMMENDED RESOURCES
Safety	Careful attention to household baby hazards

🕐 15 MINUTES   MONTH ⑪

ACTIVITY 4

Babies are fascinated by the simplest and most mundane things we take for granted as adults. Take eggs, for example. Retrieving a pan, cracking an egg, stirring it, turning on the stove, and creating an edible egg is like an act of magic to a baby. Next time you make eggs for breakfast, sit on the floor and show baby what happens when you crack an egg. Let him see you execute each step in the process and describe in detail what you are doing and why you are doing it. Chances are good that your baby has never seen a cracked egg ooze out it's yolky goodness and be turned into a meal.

DEVELOPMENTAL FOCUS	RECOMMENDED RESOURCES
Cause and Effect, Cognitive Development	Eggs

10 MINUTES   MONTH 11

ACTIVITY 5

Go to the thrift store (or Craigslist) and buy an old instrument – a ukulele, guitar, bongo, triangle, cowbell, keyboard... it doesn't matter. While singing your nursery rhymes strum the guitar and do a dance. While listening to the radio, bust out your cowbell (or pots and pans) and play along with your percussion instrument. Your baby will see you having fun and will embrace your love of music along with you. It doesn't matter if you're any good or even if you know how to play. Baby doesn't know what a master pianist does or doesn't sound like. Just laugh and have fun! Be sure to encourage baby to play along.

DEVELOPMENTAL
FOCUS

RECOMMENDED
RESOURCES

**Creativity, Musical
Development**

Old instruments

60 MINUTES   MONTH **11**

ACTIVITY 6

Disrupt your schedule! Stay late at a friends house. Go to dinner on a weeknight. Linger around the park for a few more swings or slides. As a caregiver you've likely worked very hard to create a predictable sleeping, eating, bathing, etc. schedule for your baby. This is a good thing! But it's also important to enjoy life and teach baby how to adjust to unpredictability. Give it a try!

DEVELOPMENTAL FOCUS

RECOMMENDED RESOURCES

Social Skills   Lost in the moment

2 MINUTES   MONTH 11

ACTIVITY 7

Learning concepts is tough, and it takes time at this age. Work on teaching "soft", "gentle", "hot", "cold", etc. through repetition. For example, while out on a walk or at the store, stop to look at the soft petals of a flower, and show baby how you gently stroke them. While lighting a candle, show baby the hot flame and that it can cause an ouchie. When getting ice from the freezer, let baby feel the cold air and the cold ice cube. Say the word as you illustrate the concept.

DEVELOPMENTAL FOCUS	RECOMMENDED RESOURCES
Language Development	Flower, candle, match, ice

_____

_____

_____

120 MINUTES   MONTH 11

ACTIVITY 8

Date night!! Finding time for you and your partner is getting harder and harder. With work, house chores, grocery shopping, paying the bills, taking care of baby, and on, and on, we often lose focus of our friends and family. It's worth the effort to get a babysitter so you can steal away for an hour or two for some alone time or romantic time.

DEVELOPMENTAL
FOCUS

Sanity for Mom and
Dad

RECOMMENDED
RESOURCES

Babysitter

_____
_____
_____

5 MINUTES   MONTH (11)

ACTIVITY 9

Stack a bunch of blocks to make a tower. Let your baby knock it down. Then stack the tower again, and let her knock it down again. Do this a few times. Next, play the role of a dragon who is protecting the castle and have baby be the knight who was sent to destroy it (girls can be knights, too!). Be sure to make your best dragon noises and flap your dragon wings. And let baby win every now and then. ;-)

DEVELOPMENTAL FOCUS	RECOMMENDED RESOURCES
Motor Skills	Blocks

○ 3 MINUTES   MONTH ⑪

ACTIVITY 10

Throughout the day today, focus on looking up. We focus so much on what's directly in front of our feet. Switch it up. While out and about, point to planes in the sky, birds in the trees, the moon behind the clouds. Talk about who might be on the plane, what the birds are doing in the trees, and why the moon is ducking and diving behind the clouds.

DEVELOPMENTAL FOCUS	RECOMMENDED RESOURCES
Awareness of the World	Neck muscles

_____

_____

_____

2 MINUTES   MONTH **11**

ACTIVITY 11

Today give your child 3 big hugs at random times for no reason at all & tell them you love them. Ask them to surprise mommy or daddy with a hug and say I love you, too!

DEVELOPMENTAL
FOCUS

RECOMMENDED
RESOURCES

Family Bonding

Hugs

15 MINUTES   MONTH 11

ACTIVITY 12

Sensory processing delays – such as hearing and sight – also impact fine motor development. Your physician can check on these types of things and give you input if you happen to notice anything. And you can do some simple tests, too. Does your child turn her head when you say her name? Can she locate objects on pages of books? Take notes if you think something is off and write down your questions ahead of your next doctors visit so you can discuss with your physician.

DEVELOPMENTAL FOCUS

Fine Motor Skills

RECOMMENDED RESOURCES

Observations and note taking

8 MINUTES   MONTH 11

ACTIVITY 13

Create a fun challenge for your child by setting up an obstacle course. Use pillows and cushions from the couch and blankets and other soft, lumpy things for your child to crawl or walk over. You can put their favorite toy at the end of the course so they earn a "prize" for their achievement.

DEVELOPMENTAL
FOCUS

RECOMMENDED
RESOURCES

Gross Motor Skills

Pillows and blankets

Chris Drew, Ph.D.

⏱ 2 MINUTES   MONTH ⑪

ACTIVITY 14

Don't down play goo goo ga ga. It is an important step of language development called babbling. She won't be speaking full sentences yet, but that doesn't mean you can't understand what she's communicating. In babbling you notice that your child's patterns mimic moods and modes in her life. Encourage babbling by doing it with your baby. Da da da. Ma ma ma. La la la. Ha ha ha.

DEVELOPMENTAL FOCUS

Language Development

RECOMMENDED RESOURCES

Your voice

2 MINUTES   MONTH 11

ACTIVITY 15

It's never too early to start working on phonics. Sing the A B Cs by sounding out each of the letters phonetically. For example, sing, "Ah, Ba, Ck, Du, Eh, Fuh, Guh, Hh, Eye, Juh, Kuh, Ll, Um, Nn, Ohh,"... etc.

DEVELOPMENTAL FOCUS

Language Development

RECOMMENDED RESOURCES

Your voice

10 MINUTES   MONTH **11**

ACTIVITY 16

Does your baby love to touch and pull, tug and yank while you're reading books? Don't fight it. Encourage it! Get tactile books that have a cornucopia of textures. Show baby how to flip the pages and have him take turns flipping the pages.

DEVELOPMENTAL FOCUS

RECOMMENDED RESOURCES

Pre-literacy Skills, Fine Motor Skills

Tactile books

_____

_____

_____

10 MINUTES   MONTH **11**

ACTIVITY 17

It's easy to fall into the trap of giving baby girls dolls or pink-colored toys to play with and giving boys trucks or blue-colored toys to play with. Try not to pigeonhole your baby by their gender. Switch it up. Introduce building blocks to your daughter. Bring your son into the kitchen to help prepare a meal. Play catch with your girl. Play an instrument with your boy.

DEVELOPMENTAL FOCUS

Social Development

RECOMMENDED RESOURCES

Different Colors

⏱ 1 MINUTES   MONTH 11

ACTIVITY 18

For no reason, walk up behind and give your partner a hug. Offer your wife a back rub. Present your husband with a cookie. Call your sister or text your brother to tell them you love them. Post something thoughtful on your bestie's Facebook page. Send a positive karmic ripple into the world of your loved ones. You'll feel good that you did it.

DEVELOPMENTAL FOCUS	RECOMMENDED RESOURCES
Family Bonding	A positive thought

⏱ 3 MINUTES   MONTH ⑪

ACTIVITY 19

Introduce some new and creative sounds by freestyling your favorite nursery rhyme. Old McDonald had a funky farm. All the animals say, "Heeey. Ohhh. Heeey. Ohhh." Old McDonald had a funky farm. All the plants say, "Sun and grow. Sun and grow." Make it up as you go! What types of animals can you think of besides horses, pigs, and cows? See if you can find a new animal, like a meerkat, a bison, an impala, or even a dragon! And what about the plants? Can they talk and sing?

DEVELOPMENTAL FOCUS

Language Development

RECOMMENDED RESOURCES

Creativity

_____
_____
_____

Chris Drew, Ph.D.

◷ 3 MINUTES   MONTH ⑪

ACTIVITY 20

Do 10 pushups and eat an apple.

DEVELOPMENTAL
FOCUS

Health and fitness for Mom and Dad

RECOMMENDED
RESOURCES

The ground and an apple

_____
_____
_____

2 MINUTES   MONTH 11

ACTIVITY 21

Introduce and talk about concepts "fast" and "slow". Throw a scarf or tissue or balloon in the air and watch it float down. Talk about how slowly it comes down. Now toss a stuffed animal or pillow in the air and talk about how quickly it falls to the ground. You can do this with a ball by rolling it across the floor slow or fast. Watch cars as they go zooooming past or creeping slowly by. Use hand motions as you say the words.

DEVELOPMENTAL FOCUS	RECOMMENDED RESOURCES
Language Development	Tissue, ball, scarf

_____

_____

_____

🕐 5 MINUTES   MONTH 11

ACTIVITY 22

Research shows laughter triggers chemicals in the brain that heighten memory. Every now and then, when talking with your child, use funny voices and silly faces. The goal is to laugh together. What other fun and funny things can you do to make memories?

DEVELOPMENTAL
FOCUS

RECOMMENDED
RESOURCES

Cognitive Development, Happiness

Smiles and laughter

_____

_____

_____

20 MINUTES   MONTH 11

ACTIVITY 23

Grab the stroller and head out for a walk. While walking around your neighborhood point out plants, houses, signs, and cars and say the color. Point at houses and buildings and discuss who or what may be inside. Talk about your environment while walking around as a way to build awareness of surroundings, to highlight the colors around you, and even as a way to instill a sense of direction.

DEVELOPMENTAL FOCUS

Language Development, Spatial Awareness

RECOMMENDED RESOURCES

Your feet and a stroller

1 WEEK   MONTH 11

ACTIVITY 24

What are some activities that normally only Mom does with baby? Does Mommy always do the feeding? Does Mommy usually change the diapers? Does Mommy usually put baby to bed every night? Try switching it up for an entire week. Have Daddy do dinner-time feeding. Daddy and baby can be the ones who go to the grocery store or put baby down for bed. While it may be challenging to your routines, it will be a nice switch for both parents, and it will be good for baby to bond in a slightly different way. Try to do this for a full week.

DEVELOPMENTAL FOCUS	RECOMMENDED RESOURCES
Daddy–baby Bonding	Daddy and baby

PARENT'S NOTES
Advice from Our Readers
MONTH ELEVEN

RUBBING THE MOM OFF

Kendall B., Mom to Jackson, Cambria, CA

Yesterday, I apologized, rather profusely, to a co-worker while giving him a ride in my mom-infested, what-I-considered-to-be-embarrassing car. After rushing to move all the toys (and yes a soiled diaper in a plastic bag from two days previous) from the passenger side of the car, throwing my make-up into the car seat, and chucking running shoes, and other personal objects to the back-seat like a drug smuggler, I proceeded to spend our 5 minute car ride justifying to him the state of my unwashed, unvacuumed crap-filled mom-mobile. I was embarrassed.

But my embarrassment bothered me. And today I realized why. I am supermom - I have a full time job, I pump, I pack lunch daily, I grocery shop for our family, I support my husband, see my family, have some resemblance of a social life, plan vacations, balance our budget, bond with our daughter, empty the dishwasher, do the laundry a respectable amount, and, perhaps most importantly, I have managed to stay (mostly) sane for nearly the last year.

Is my car a complete disaster? Yes. Does doing my make-up on-the-go get me nearly an extra hour every week with my daughter? Yes. I do not need to "Rub the Mom off" before I go to work. I am both a dedicated employee and a mother. Next time I will embrace these new facts of my life and I will not apologize for being a supermom. I will strap a cape to the back of my mom-mobile and explain to my co-workers that this is what having it all looks like. And I will proudly spend that extra hour a week enjoying every possible waking moment with my daughter - teaching her about the world, loving her until my heart explodes.

~ Kendall B., Cambria, CA

PARENT WIN

Essential Activities
To Nurture Smarter Kids

THE FIRST YEAR

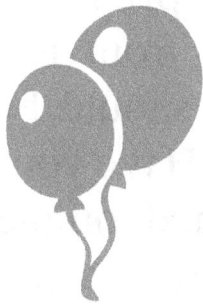

MONTH

20 MINUTES   MONTH 12

ACTIVITY 1

At this age baby is eating more table foods. Even though his primary source of nutrition still comes from formula or breast milk your baby should be receiving balanced nutrition. Have you spoken to your doctor, researched online, or discussed with other parents the best way to be filling out your baby's diet.

DEVELOPMENTAL FOCUS	RECOMMENDED RESOURCES
Nutrition	Nutrition research

_____

_____

_____

5 MINUTES   MONTH 12

ACTIVITY 2

Every Saturday and Sunday we walk to the corner Starbucks to get an extra hot, vinti, skinny, vanilla latte. Madison sees us with our Starbucks cups and she wants what Mommy and Daddy have. The barista will hand her a lid so she can feel like she's participating with her own Starbucks drink. Be aware that your eating and drinking habits are the same habits that will develop into desires for your baby. What are the treats you indulge in and how do you communicate that this is a special drink for Mommy and Daddy?

DEVELOPMENTAL
FOCUS

Habit Formation

RECOMMENDED
RESOURCES

Good habits

_____

_____

_____

20 MINUTES   MONTH 12

ACTIVITY 3

After you put the kids to bed take a few moments to be still and have some alone time. Close your eyes, breath deeply and listen to soothing music. You deserve it!

DEVELOPMENTAL
FOCUS

RECOMMENDED
RESOURCES

**Mommy and Daddy
sanity**

Relaxation

_____

_____

_____

12 MINUTES   MONTH 12

ACTIVITY 4

Explore new foods with new textures and tastes. Even though your baby may have his favorites fruits or vegetables, switch up and try something new this week. When eating bananas describe how they are sticky, slippery, and mushy in your mouth. While eating a cooked carrot describe where the carrot came from and how you prepared it (or how Gerber made it ;-) so that your baby could eat it.

DEVELOPMENTAL FOCUS	RECOMMENDED RESOURCES
Language Development, Nutrition	Whatever is for dinner

10 MINUTES   MONTH 12

ACTIVITY 5

While folding clothes, sit on the floor and toss all the unfolded onesies, shirts, and pants into the air and let them fall on you and your baby. Weee! It's raining clothes! When a shirt falls on your baby's head, play peek-a-boo. Where's baby?! It's a game to play to make folding clothes a family activity and turn a chore into a bit of fun. Be sure to get dad in on the action so he can help.

DEVELOPMENTAL FOCUS

Fun!

RECOMMENDED RESOURCES

Clean laundry

🕐 20 MINUTES   MONTH 12

ACTIVITY 6

It's easy to turn a short walk around the block into a learning expedition. Stop to feel the bark of a tree and describe the rough (or smooth) texture. Bend over to look at a flowering bush and feel the soft petals and smell the fragrant scent. Show baby a thorny bush and explain how it can hurt and cause an ouchie. Look in the sky for birds sitting on power lines and explain the tweeting or crowing. You don't have to be on safari or at a zoo for baby to learn cool things about her world.

DEVELOPMENTAL FOCUS	RECOMMENDED RESOURCES
Language Development	**Your neighborhood**

2 MINUTES   MONTH 12

ACTIVITY 7

Baby is getting better and better with solid foods, but still you need to be cautious of choking hazard foods such as grapes, hot dogs, some berries, or other small foods that could cause your baby to choke. Grapes are perfectly sized for adults, but you may need to cut the grapes into halves for baby.

DEVELOPMENTAL   RECOMMENDED
FOCUS   RESOURCES

Safety   Cutting Knife

_____

_____

_____

40 MINUTES   MONTH 12

ACTIVITY 8

Got out to dinner with your baby. This could be your corner Starbucks or Ruth's Chris. As with all outings, your baby is watching you. Use this eating out occasion to demonstrate good manners, healthy eating habits, and other behaviors that you want baby to have. While out to eat at a restaurant, demonstrate good etiquette and show baby how you put the napkin in your lap. Describe why you put your cell phone away to engage in conversation with the others in your party. If baby has a meltdown, calmly, but sternly, explain that we don't behave that way at dinner.

DEVELOPMENTAL FOCUS	RECOMMENDED RESOURCES
Social Skills	Restaurant

3 MINUTES   MONTH 12

ACTIVITY 9

At this age discipline or telling the baby what not to do is not as important as teaching the baby what to do. But how you instruct your baby is the most important thing. Look her in the eye, use a serious (but calm) voice, and provide her with the corrective guidance that she needs. You'll have to do this many, many more times. So patience is key. Remember, it's okay to go back to laughing and having fun after the teachable moment. ...as long as baby isn't throwing food all over the place ;-)

DEVELOPMENTAL   RECOMMENDED
FOCUS   RESOURCES

Social Skills, Respect   **Patience**

_____

_____

_____

5 MINUTES   MONTH 12

As a counter to the previous activity, remember that at this age, when it comes to appropriate behavior, baby needs to learn what TO DO. Positive reinforcement, modeling, and encouraging correct behaviors is much more effective than attempting to correct bad behaviors. While baby is getting older and can learn what not to do, she is still a baby. And a big part of being a baby is to play around and try EVERYTHING!

DEVELOPMENTAL FOCUS	RECOMMENDED RESOURCES
Social Skills	Patience (and more patience)

10 MINUTES   MONTH 12

ACTIVITY 11

For the past 11 months it may seem like your primary job as a parent has been to do everything in your power to keep your baby from killing herself. She's constantly trying to fling herself down steps, crawl off the side of Mommy and Daddy's bed, drink whatever poisons are under the sink, eating squirrel poop, and a million other things. So naturally at this age it is common that baby hears more "no", "don't" and other negatives more so than they do positive reinforcement of what to do. Be conscientious of positive versus negative feedback to your baby. Research shows that the more positive language we can surround baby with the more stimulated they are. So instead of saying "No, don't do that" try saying, "Let's go over here and explore a better option."

Chris Drew, Ph.D.

DEVELOPMENTAL FOCUS	RECOMMENDED RESOURCES
Language Development, Cognitive Development	**Positive language**

2 MINUTES   MONTH 12

ACTIVITY 12

Sometimes it will seem to your child that the activity from which you're trying to remove her is more fun than any other thing in the world. At these times play up and act like the preferred activity is so much more fun. "Hey Madison, check out this rattle in my hand. Woohoo! This is way more awesome than that hand soap you're trying to drink! Let's come over here and party with me and the rattle!"

DEVELOPMENTAL FOCUS	RECOMMENDED RESOURCES
Safety	Enthusiasm and distracting activity

_____

_____

_____

7 MINUTES   MONTH 12

ACTIVITY 13

Instead of saying, "No. No. Don't play with the cleaner." Say, "Here, play with the Tupperware." Offering positive alternatives is a good habit to get into. Try to avoid stifling exploration, and instead try to direct your baby's exploration.

DEVELOPMENTAL FOCUS	RECOMMENDED RESOURCES
Language Development, Cognitive Development	Positive language

30-90 MINUTES   MONTH ⑫

ACTIVITY 14

By this age some kids are sleeping through the night (if you're lucky) and taking two naps throughout the day. Your baby is nearly 1 year old and isn't napping the same way he did when he came home for the first couple months, but he still needs lots of rest.

DEVELOPMENTAL FOCUS	RECOMMENDED RESOURCES
Growth and Physical Development	Naps

_____

_____

_____

ACTIVITY 15

Do baby's dream? Is she forming memories yet? Well, baby can certainly remember familiar caregivers she hasn't seen for a month. But will she remember things 12 years from now. That's debate for the specialists. But just be aware that as your child develops memory he or she may develop dreams throughout the night. And it is possible that the dreams may wake your baby. She'll go back to sleep most of the time. But that's fun fact to be aware of if you hear her startle in the night.

DEVELOPMENTAL FOCUS

Cognitive Development

RECOMMENDED RESOURCES

Awareness

30 MINUTES   MONTH 12

ACTIVITY 16

Sleeping through the night is considered eight hours of continuous sleep. However, sleeping patterns will change if your child is sick, cutting teeth, or has a change in his routine. This can be exhausting and frustrating for parents. But make mental notes of how baby reacts to disruptions to his routines and make a plan for how to mitigate the disruption (for the sake of your own sanity!). For example, if you know that you are traveling and that baby cannot sleep well when in the same room as Mommy (which is the case with Madison), then think about having a strategic place to put her crib. Yes, we have in fact put her Pack and Play in the hotel bathroom before. (Be sure to make sure there are no chords or other hazards she can get her hands on from inside the crib.)

Chris Drew, Ph.D.

DEVELOPMENTAL FOCUS	RECOMMENDED RESOURCES
Mommy and Daddy sanity	**Planning and strategy**

_____

_____

_____

20 MINUTES   MONTH 12

ACTIVITY 17

Physical activity for Mom and Dad is important to staying healthy and burning off stress and tension. Go for a walk or a jog by yourself, or do some stretching or pushups to circulate the blood. Mom and Dad need a good night's rest too! Being physically active can help you rest better at night.

DEVELOPMENTAL FOCUS	RECOMMENDED RESOURCES
Mommy and Daddy health and sanity	Time

60 MINUTES   MONTH 12

ACTIVITY 18

This week, as you prepare for your baby's first birthday, reflect on all you have accomplished as a parent and the amazing development that has taken place with your baby. What are some of the most cherished moments from this 1st year? Be sure to relish in this time. Not only has your baby grown, but so have you. You should be proud of yourself and all you've done with your new role in the most important job you'll ever have as a caregiver to your baby.

DEVELOPMENTAL FOCUS	RECOMMENDED RESOURCES
Mommy and Daddy reflection	Pictures, notes, memory book

30 MINUTES   MONTH 12

ACTIVITY 19

Setting goals is important. What are some goals you would like to set for yourself as a parent for this next year? Write them down. It can be a simple goal like trying to have 1 play date each month or something big like getting a promotion at work. Make a game plan for how you will actually execute on achieving your goal. What steps will you take? Will you dedicate 15 minutes a week to researching play date ideas? Will you dedicate one night per week of working on a side project? Whatever it is, write it down!

DEVELOPMENTAL FOCUS

Mommy and Daddy personal development

RECOMMENDED RESOURCES

Paper and pen

2 MINUTES   MONTH ⑫

ACTIVITY 20

All the daily activities in this book are grounded in child development research. And hopefully they have helped you juggle the daily challenges of parenting. But it's important to know, whether you've done 10 activities or 200 activities from this book, it's okay! You love your baby and it shows. You're doing a great job! This reference book has hopefully helped give a lil extra support along the way.

(And, by the way, we've written an activity book for you to use with your 1 year old. Go out and pick up a copy for your Kindle, your coffee table, or your porcelain throne. ;-)

DEVELOPMENTAL   RECOMMENDED
FOCUS   RESOURCES

General Development   1 year old activity
                                  book

335

10 MINUTES   MONTH 12

ACTIVITY 21

Over this past year you have done a great job of establishing some positive routines with your baby. What's the best routine you have? What is one habit or routine you want to get rid of in this next year? Baby is much to young to do anything like this – and will be too young for several more years – but remember that you are exhibiting habits, values, and behaviors that your baby will imitate throughout her life. You are setting the example. Even though baby won't understand, you can show her what you're writing and what it means. (Plus, research shows that when we make goals and then tell others about them we develop an increased sense of responsibility to deliver!)

Chris Drew, Ph.D.

DEVELOPMENTAL FOCUS	RECOMMENDED RESOURCES
Mommy and Daddy personal development	Reflection

_____

_____

_____

5 MINUTES   MONTH 12

ACTIVITY 22

Congratulations Mom and Dad, you did it! You've made it through the first year with your new baby. Now it's time to look forward to another exciting year of development and milestones. Be sure to pick up Volume 2 for your family to use with your 1 year old! And if you're feeling up to it, send us a note with feedback. We would love to hear from you.

DEVELOPMENTAL FOCUS

RECOMMENDED RESOURCES

Congratulations!

Many, many pats on the back!

Chris Drew, Ph.D.

PARENT'S NOTES
Advice from Our Readers
MONTH TWELVE

IS MY DAUGHTER BORED?

Mary Ann S., Mom to Keesha, Brentwood, CA

As I have watched my daughter grow and explore new and interesting things, I have often found myself wondering - is she bored? Do I have enough age-appropriate toys for her? Do I read to her enough? Is she getting enough stimulation? Too much stimulation? How can I tell? And if she is bored, what should I do with her so she learns at the best pace possible? I don't want a million toys strewn about my house (hate it!) and I certainly don't want to spoil her. But what is the best for her?

As I've navigated this question over the first year of her life, often over-correcting (did she just pass out in her high chair in the middle of eating dinner?!), my lesson has been that more than toys, she enjoys activities with people. She loves new surroundings, with a mix of discovering things in and around our home. Everything is new to her. And having me get down with her at her level and appreciate all those new things from her perspective keeps her engaged and learning.

When she's looking intently at the ground, it's only when I bend over to see that she is very closely studying ants walk in a row. When I start to tell her what the ants are and what they are doing, she excitedly reaches out to touch them. We discovered lighting the candles in our home with matches because I sat to explore with her as she grabbed at the candle (now one of her favorite activities). We taught her to smell by stopping to look with her at the high-contrast, colorful flowers on our walks when she would point them out. She learned what "hot" means (now her favorite word) because each time Mommy had a fresh Starbucks coffee in her hand she naturally wanted to hold it too.

Does she need age appropriate toys? Absolutely. But instead of stressing about which toys and how many to buy, I think I'll take that internet research time and get down on the floor, wherever she is and teach her about the world that she is experiencing and exploring.

~ Mary Ann S., Brentwood, CA

EVERYTHING IS WONDERFUL, YET STILL I WORRY

Nikki S., Mom to Douglas, San Jose, CA

I am blissfully happy, my husband is kind, capable, and helpful, and, most importantly, my baby is wonderful. Despite not having family who live close by or much support outside of the three of us, I feel I've had an easy experience as a first-time-mom. Sure, there have been some typical, short-lived, mildly difficult times – like waking up every three hours to breastfeed in the early days and a few fussy evenings early on when I'd be counting the minutes for daddy to get home from work. That aside, my baby slept through the night from around 2 months of age. We've had no difficulties with breastfeeding, milk supply, or eventual weaning, and he's a good eater. He has always been content, 'independent', securely-attached, and happy to go to others. He's been perfectly healthy aside from a few colds, teething (so far) came and went relatively unnoticed, and developmental milestones have been reached within appropriate timeframes.

When my mama friends talk about how difficult "momming" can be, I keep my mouth shut. It's been easy for me. The extrinsic factors have to play a role. For example, I haven't had to go back to work. I get enough sleep. And I haven't had to deal with health issues for my baby or me. Or it may be partly intrinsic: I'm relaxed and don't tend to sweat the small stuff, nor does my husband. Is my baby's easygoing spirit a result of nurture or nature or both? Whatever it may be, here's the worry that's always been on my mind… will it last?!

From when my son was just a couple of months old, I couldn't help wondering whether he would continue to be a happy and easy boy. Whenever I shared with anybody the fact that things were going smoothly, I'd consistently add the words "so far" or "who knows how long it will last" or "we'll see what change the future brings". Well, my son's first birthday has come and gone, and he's still a delight in every way, just about all the time! He now has a baby sister on the way. Yet worry clouds my mind constantly. I have to stop myself from thinking and saying "he may yet turn into a terrible two" or "his sister is likely to be a nightmare because we couldn't possibly be so lucky again".

Well, maybe we could be so lucky! Maybe we are that blessed! Maybe we have great genes or are doing everything inadvertently right! I haven't quite stopped wondering or questioning, but I'm trying. I am attempting to anticipate my son continues to be wonderful and that our daughter is just as wonderful. Perhaps it's human nature, and most especially true for parents, that when we love something so much, there is always a fear that it will be taken away in some form or another. But, I'm getting better and better at trusting and enjoying every present moment.

~ Nikki S., San Jose, CA

Photo by Rhee Bevere

ABOUT THE AUTHOR

As a professor and education researcher, Chris Drew, Ph.D, has placed his focus on learning and literacy, which has led to groundbreaking innovations in early childhood education technology. These efforts have helped thousands of families across the country and the world.

His new educational series, *Parent Win: Essential Activities To Nurture Smarter Kids*, is the culmination of numerous studies. Working with many leading childhood educational organizations, universities and researchers, Drew has developed, tested and refined the values of this series. He is the founding Director of the Micro-Credentialing Initiative at Digital Promise, a Congressionally authorized education think tank. He also founded Parent University, a digital parent empowerment community that coaches parents to be their child's best teacher.

Born in Tennessee and raised in Illinois, Drew's Midwestern ethic permeates the spirit of his work. The eldest of four, he comes from a family of educators, coaches, and development experts. Most proudly, he is a husband and the father of a daughter.

Over the past decade Drew has focused on his child development research, driven and motivated by the impact of his efforts to empower moms and dads. He recalls, "The most transcendent moment of my entire professional life was when I received a heart-wrenching response from a parent from one of my early pilot studies. She was so grateful, so happy. It was a simple exchange between us, but it sticks with me still."

The author has earned advanced degrees from Temple University and Southern Illinois University, and an Executive Education certification from the Stanford Graduate School of Business.

Chris Drew lives with his wife and daughter in Silicon Valley, where he and his family regularly immerse themselves in the natural wonders of California.

Contact the Author at:
Chris.Drew.Books@gmail.com

Mom and Dad!
Tell us what you have been learning!

Share your insights and observations to help
new parents across the globe.

Submit Your
PARENT'S NOTES

We hope to include your words and advice
in the next edition of this book!

Send to:
Chris.Drew.Books@gmail.com

COMING SOON!

Werd Factory Books Presents

New Activities for the Second Year of Your Growing and Learning Baby

PARENT WIN

*Essential Activities
To Nurture Smarter Kids*

THE SECOND YEAR

Chris Drew, Ph.D.

Werd Factory Books

PARENT WIN

*Essential Activities
To Nurture Smarter Kids*

THE FIRST YEAR

Chris Drew, Ph.D.

www.ingramcontent.com/pod-product-compliance
Lightning Source LLC
Chambersburg PA
CBHW070339090426
42733CB00009B/1233